SICILY

by RUSSELL KING

DAVID & CHARLES: NEWTON ABBOT

STACKPOLE BOOKS: HARRISBURG

This edition first published in 1973
in Great Britain by
David & Charles (Holdings) Limited Newton Abbot Devon
in the United States in 1973 by
Stackpole Books Harrisburg Pa

ISBN 0 7153 6359 X *(Great Britain)*
ISBN 0 8117 1531 0 *(United States)*

*Set in eleven on thirteen point Baskerville
and printed in Great Britain
by Latimer Trend & Company Ltd*

THE ISLANDS SERIES

SICILY

THE ISLANDS SERIES

* Published in the United States by Stackpole
† Published in the United States by David & Charles
‡ Distributed in Australia by Wren

CONTENTS

ILLUSTRATIONS

ILLUSTRATIONS

All photographs by courtesy of the Italian State Tourist Office except those marked with an asterisk which are by courtesy of *The Geographical Magazine.*

MAPS AND DIAGRAMS

A Sicily in the Central Mediterranean

1 HISTORICAL AND GEOGRAPHICAL PERSPECTIVES

ONLY 3 kilometres of shallow sea divides the 'kicking boot' of the Italian mainland from Sicily at its toe. Yet, as the visitor quickly discovers, this narrow stretch of water separates two culturally distinct worlds. The island's long, dramatic history has been shaped not by its proximity to Italy but by its location at the centre of the Mediterranean, on the southern fringes of Europe and only 150km from North Africa. This is also reflected in the transitional features of the landscape. The mountains behind Messina will remind the visitor arriving off the ferry of the woods and hills of northern Europe; the wide open spaces of central and western Sicily resemble the Spanish *meseta*, and the eastern part of the island, with its olive groves, terracing and dry-stone walls, are reminiscent of Greece and the Aegean. To the south, the long rolling hills and dunes, utterly treeless for the most part, foreshadow the approach to North Africa.

Sicily has been a perpetual meeting place of cultures and a battleground for armies. There are prehistoric and native tombs in their thousands; Greek temples and theatres as magnificent as those of Greece itself; Roman villas, Byzantine mosaics, Arab cloisters, Norman castles and some hundreds of baroque Spanish churches. The inhabitants too reflect a mixed heritage, for the physique of the islanders shows traces of Greek, Arab, Norman and Spaniard, although in ascribing the occasional fair-haired, blue-eyed Sicilian to a Norman origin one should not forget the sexual perambulations of the occupying forces during the last war, a fact which also explains the occasional darker-skinned Sicilian with somewhat negroid features.

The island's most obvious historical role has been as a bridge between Europe and Africa, and enthusiastic Sicilians today talk of the island as a bridgehead between the Common Market and the rapidly expanding countries of North Africa. At one time or another Sicily has played host to most of the great Mediterranean civilisations and powers. It was a centre of prehistoric trading; it flourished in classical Greek times and later became the centre of the Islamic Mediterranean empire. Under the Spaniards it became a far-flung and forgotten province, neglected by the passing of the mainstream of world history beyond Europe and the Mediterranean to the New World. The Industrial Revolution too passed the island by. Unification with Italy in 1860 brought few benefits; indeed the bitter joke about the Italian boot kicking Sicily dates from this time.

At one time called Trinacria, because of its roughly triangular shape, Sicily was named after the Siculi, an ancient pre-Greek tribe that once lived there. The largest island in the Mediterranean—25,709sq km—it is surrounded by a constellation of minor islands, with a collective area of about 270sq km and a population of 35,581. Sicily's population has been continually increasing and by 1971 was approaching 5 million. From 1 million in 1501 it reached 2 million by 1814 and 2,392,000 in the first national census of 1861. Censuses have since recorded 3,530,000 in 1901; 3,897,000 in 1931; 4,486,000 in 1951, and 4,721,000 in 1961. Throughout the past hundred years Sicily has contained about 10 per cent of the Italian population.

Administratively the island is divided into nine provinces, whose population and area characteristics are shown in Table 1, and 380 communes. Each commune commonly consists of a single village and its territory, but a number of communes, especially in the provinces of Messina and Trapani, are com-

Table 1

SICILY: AREA AND POPULATION CHARACTERISTICS
OF THE PROVINCES (1961 CENSUS)

Province	Area sq km	Population	Density per sq km	Number of communes
Agrigento	3,042	472,945	155	43
Caltanissetta	2,104	302,513	144	22
Catania	3,552	893,542	252	55
Enna	2,562	229,126	89	20
Messina	3,247	685,260	211	105
Palermo	5,016	1,111,397	222	81
Ragusa	1,614	252,769	157	12
Siracusa	2,109	345,777	164	19
Trapani	2,462	427,672	174	23
	25,708	4,721,001	184	380

posed of two or more settlements, the total number of villages in the island being above 800. Villages are particularly small in Messina province (average size 1,200 inhabitants), but are much larger in central and southern parts of the island (average of 12,000 in Ragusa province). Less than 5 per cent of the population live in scattered settlements and farms, though the proportion is 20 per cent in the province of Messina. The provinces have little correspondence to natural or geographical regions but, very roughly, western Sicily is made up of Palermo, Trapani and Agrigento provinces; Enna, Caltanissetta and Ragusa make up the central part of the island, and Messina, Catania and Siracusa the eastern region.

UNIFICATION WITH ITALY

Union with Italy in 1860 is interpreted by Sicilians as the cause of all the island's current social and economic ills, and by north Italians as the first step towards bringing civilisation to a barbarous island. The immediate post-Unification period was remarkable for the ignorance that prevailed about the real conditions of life in Sicily and in southern Italy in general, for few politicians ventured south of Rome. The working structure of the new Italy was heavily weighted against a region like Sicily. The location of the government in the north, the sources of industrial power being discovered in the Po Plain, the nearness of the north to the progressive areas and big markets of Europe, and the removal of protectionism for southern industry all led to a rapid decline of Palermo as an industrial centre. The land tax took no account of the low productivity of Sicilian soil; the property tax applied to all Sicilian peasant hovels because they happened to be concentrated in villages and towns whilst it did not apply to the scattered farmsteads more characteristic of the mainland, and the food taxes weighed heavily upon an island where almost the whole of personal incomes went on satisfying basic necessities. Symptomatic of local unrest and hatred of the government was the Palermo revolt of 1866, an uprising brutally put down by 40,000 troops and treated as a purely military matter, instead of as an indicator of fundamental malaise.

The persistence of an oppressive social structure within the island was another important factor. The landowning class was overwhelmingly dominant socially, economically and politically. A few hundred people owned over half the land in Sicily. With an electorate of only 1 per cent, the landlords and their retainers were virtually the only voters, blocking attempts at reform—of education, for instance—which would have led to wider enfranchisement.

Official and semi-official surveys of conditions in Sicily were in fact made, but few northern decision-makers bothered to read such weighty tomes. What did begin to change people's state of knowledge were the 'realist' writings of two of Sicily's most famous authors, Verga and Pirandello, and the positive action of the islanders themselves. Up to 1914 some 1½ million Sicilians emigrated, a dramatic exposure of the island's poverty and overpopulation. Peasant and miners' unions, called *fasci*,

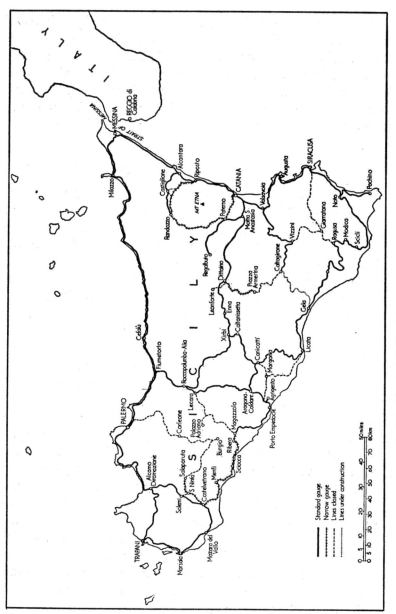

B The Island of Sicily: Principal Towns and Railways

were formed from 1889 on, and pursued activist policies of squatting on the big estates and striking in the mines. Banditry flourished in the west of the island, and Catania became noted as a centre of socialism. In the interwar period, Mussolini stamped out banditry and outlawed left-wing political groups, but the same phenomena returned after fascism, indicating that nothing in the Sicilian system had really changed for the better.

THE STRUGGLE TO PRESERVE REGIONAL IDENTITY

Unification brought a progressive Italianisation of the island, which reached its greatest extent under the fascist regime with the centralisation of all administration in Rome and the drive to eradicate regional cultures and dialects. But a certain separatist element has always been present. After the Allied occupation of Sicily in 1943, a Separatist Party emerged, with its own army in which the famous bandit Giuliano was a colonel. Pressure for independence was so great that the island was hastily granted regional autonomy in May 1946.

So Sicily now has its own regional government within the Republic of Italy. It works via the regional assembly, or Sicilian parliament, which meets in the Royal Palace in Palermo and consists of ninety members elected by universal suffrage for the various constituencies for a period of four years each. The ninety deputies in turn elect the regional cabinet of eight ministers and the president, one for each of the island's nine provinces. A *commissario* of the national government controls the regional government's deliberations and co-ordinates national and regional planning and administration. The region has legislative power regarding agriculture, forestry, mining, industry, commerce, public works, tourism and elementary education, and more limited decision-making powers (ie within the national legislature) regarding transport and communications, banking and insurance, higher education and social welfare.

There is no doubt that considerable economic and social

Page 17 Palermo, the capital city: (*above*) from off shore; (*below*) the gulf of Palermo showing the busy sea port

Page 18   Major cities: (*above*) Catania, Sicily's foremost commercial city, largely rebuilt since the eighteenth century. The Piazza Stesicoro and monument to Bellini; (*left*) Palermo, showing the straight line of the Via Roma

progress has been made during twenty-five years of autonomy, particularly in the early years under Sicilian presidents like Restivo, La Loggia and D'Angelo. The visitor cannot help but notice the new roads, schools and industries, and those who know the island intimately were aware of a new sense of hope and enterprise. Since 1950 the *Cassa per il Mezzogiorno*, the state agency for developing the Italian south, has poured money into Sicily, financing agricultural and industrial improvements. Especially in the more prosperous east of the island, the growing middle class live and eat well. But political intrigue is never absent from Sicilian affairs, stifling many attempts at progress or enmeshing them in a web of patronage and corruption. Cynics maintain that the only things that flourish in Sicily today are the vast bureaucracy of the regional government and the Mafia. Emigration has never ceased to be a problem and continues today; the best scholars, administrators, scientists and artists move to the more sophisticated and open societies of mainland Italy, among them Vittorini the novelist, Quasimodo the poet and the politicians Scelba, La Pira and La Malfa. Politically the complexion of the Sicilian parliament broadly reflects the centre-left character of the national government, but there has been a 30 per cent vote for the extreme left at times. The instability of the political scene is indicated by the fact that the region has had twenty-six governments in twenty-five years of autonomy.

TOURISM

It may be that much of the future of Sicily lies in tourism. Its climate is one of the island's major assets: an annual average of six hours sunshine per day and over ten hours during the period April to September. In 1970 some 300,000 foreigners and 1½ million Italians spent £13 million and about 4 million hotel-days in Sicily. In spite of the fact that tourism is one of the few sectors of the economy which is progressing, total benefit is far short of the potential. Eighty-five million people, chiefly north Europeans, spend their holidays in the Mediterranean each year. That Sicily's share of this trade is so small is due to lack of active tourist policy and also to a shortage of hotel accommodation. Although 30,000 beds are offered in hotels, pensions and inns, this accommodation is often below the standard required by the average foreign tourist, and 10,000 would be a more realistic figure. In 1970, 826 charter flights brought 53,000 visitors, mostly Germans and other continental Europeans, to the island. Only two resorts, Taormina and Cefalù, are regularly visited by British package-holiday firms. Residential tourism, involving the retirement of high income groups and the construction of villa complexes, has had little impact. Earthquakes, eruptions of Etna and the sinister image of the Mafia may have discouraged the uninitiated; but, with its abundant summer sunshine, mild winter climate, numerous empty and unpolluted beaches, as well as world-renowned archaeological and architectural treasures, it is surely only a matter of time before such tourist resources are exploited to the full.

2   SICILIAN LANDSCAPES

RELIEF AND DRAINAGE

SICILY is a young island geologically, although it contains formations of every period from Palaeozoic to Holocene, and there are a few disputed occurrences of pre-Palaeozoic rocks in the northern mountains. Sicily's mountains are part of the Tertiary Alpine-Himalayan fold system, and represent the structural continuation of the Italian Apennines and the North African Atlas ranges. Many of the uplands are formed of Mesozoic limestones. Much of the interior is of Miocene-Pliocene age and the island's famous volcanics are even more recent, continuing up to the present day. Mountains and hills cover 86 per cent of the surface, although within the mountain-hill category there is much variation. A formless jumble of hill, plateau and incised valley covers most of the interior. The principal lowland is the alluvial Plain of Catania. Other, smaller plain areas lie along the south and west coasts, with scattered pockets in river valleys and along the north coast.

Northern Sicily is dominated by a succession of mountain ranges that extend in an unbroken line from the Straits of Messina to the River Torto, standing like a high wall between the narrow north shore and the interior. Their highest peaks are all around 1,000–2,000m. The easternmost of these ranges are the Monti Peloritani, forming the backbone of the island's narrow north-east corner. Crystalline in composition (chiefly Palaeozoic schist, gneiss and granite), they are a geological continuation of

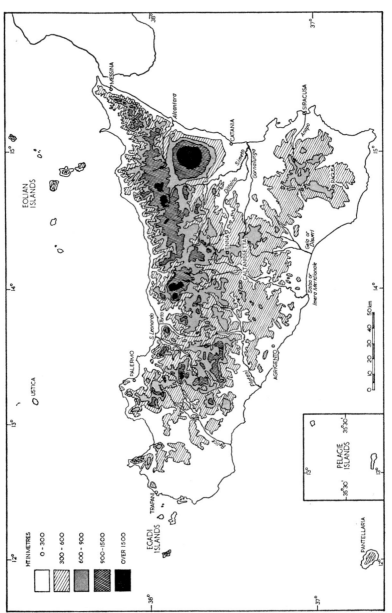

C   Relief and drainage

the Aspromonte range of southern Calabria. Beyond Novara and Mazzarra the Peloritani give way to the more extensive Tertiary sandstones and clays of the Nebrodi (or Caronie) Mountains, although the geological change is hard to distinguish topographically. The form of the Nebrodi is if anything more rounded and less jagged, but the summits are higher, the highest being M Soro (1,847m), while the Peloritani reach a maximum elevation of 1,286m (Pizzo di Vernà). The Nebrodi extend for 70km from the Novara valley as far as the Pollina valley and attain a width of about 30km. Beyond Gangi and the Pollina basin lie the Madonie, the western of the three northern mountain groups. Here the mountain range loses its longitudinal character and broadens more to a tangled mass of upland. Formed largely of limestone, although again the landscape change is not clearly visible, the Madonie are higher still. Three peaks rise just short of 2,000m; the highest being Pizzo Carbonara, 1,979m. These elevations occur where the limestone is dolomitic and hence more resistant. The Madonie range is well known for its extensive underground drainage systems, providing drinking water for Palermo and neighbouring settlements.

Beyond the line described by the Torto river, flowing north to the Tyrrhenian, and the Platani leading to the south coast, lies the region of western Sicily, a geologically confused area of clays, tufo (shelly limestone deposits) and limestone. The tufo and clays form an undulating platform ranging from sea level to about 300m, while the limestones characteristically outcrop as isolated rocks and headlands. Both sides of the Gulf of Castellammare are formed by quite impressive limestone ranges, the westernmost trending from M Inici (1,064m) to C San Vito, the easternmost containing Pizzo Montanello (964m) and the great limestone rocks that form the backdrop to Palermo (M Pellegrino 606m, M Castellaccio 890m, M Cuccio 1,050m). Another limestone outcrop, much farther west, forms the dramatic site for the hill-top town of Erice.

The central and south-western parts, bounded by the Platani and Salso rivers, form an undulating mass of uplands, tilted gently towards the south. This is a landscape of clay, sulphur, chalk and gypsum: monotonous, desolate and poor. The unstable Miocene clays are easily eroded, and great gashes of white and yellow disfigure the landscape. Between Agrigento and Caltanissetta is the *Altipiano Zolfifero* (the sulphur plateau), 1,300sq km of yellow sulphur outcrops. The relief in central Sicily trends from about 600m down towards sea level, but much of the interior lies at about 400–500m. Nowhere is 1,000m exceeded in this sea of small, rounded, bare hills, although the sedimentary rocks are known to be 8,000m thick at Caltanissetta. Local eminences, often the sites of huge clustered villages, are due to outcrops of sandstone, limestone or gypsum.

East of the Salso, roughly along the line Gangi–Enna–Piazza Armerina–Caltagirone, the plateau changes to an imperfectly defined range of uplands. These are the Monti Erei, reaching 1,000m in the neighbourhood of Enna and leading south to one of the island's most distinctive regions, the Monti Iblei, occupying the large south-eastern corner. Here the lines of relief are more tabular, due to the presence of horizontally-bedded limestones, white or yellowish in colour, overlain in the north by dark basalts. The highest point is M Lauro (986m), from which the plateaux step down southwards and from which radiate the steep-sided valleys called *cave*. North of the Iblei tablelands stretches the Plain of Catania, 430sq km, which until recently contained large areas of lake and marsh. The work of drainage and irrigation, accomplished largely under Mussolini, continues today. North of the Catania Plain, dominating the whole of eastern Sicily, looms the great cone of M Etna, built up by successive eruptions to almost 3,300m.

Large permanent rivers are non-existent, owing to the aridity of summer, the absence of perennial snow on the mountains and the geologically porous nature of much of the island's rocks.

Even the Simeto, the largest river, varies in flow from an average of only 1 cubic metre per second in summer to 2,125 in winter. Most smaller watercourses disappear altogether during the summer.

The proximity to the north coast of the island's main watershed means that the north-flowing rivers are very different in character from those flowing south. None of the numerous watercourses along the north coast, draining the Nebrodi and Peloritani ranges, exceeds 30km in length, and towards the east, as the watershed of the Peloritani approaches nearer the coast, the streams are only a few kilometres long. These short, precipitous watercourses, called *fiumare* or 'torrents', become dangerously full during the autumn rains but dwindle towards the middle of summer to mere brooks trickling down a wide expanse of stones and boulders. All along the north coast west of Termini Imerese, and down the east coast as far as Taormina, the flanks of the mountains, at intervals of about a kilometre or so, are gashed by these rather ugly *fiumare*.

West of the Torto, with the more open, compartmented relief of western Sicily and the Madonie, the rivers are longer. The San Leonardo, with its estuary at Termini Imerese, is 43km long, and the Torto itself 50km. Much larger rivers also flow into the Ionian Sea south of Taormina. The Alcantara, rising in the eastern Nebrodi near Floresta, forms the great structural valley between the Peloritani and M Etna, entering the sea just south of Taormina. The Simeto has a very similar course, rising in the same vicinity but flowing round the other side of Etna; it enters the sea in the Catanian Plain, but its estuary has changed position several times, chiefly to the south. The Dittaino and the Gornalunga join the Simeto just before its estuary, though when the plain was less extensive they had their own estuaries. Farther south, the chief river of the Iblei region is the Anapo, flowing into the sea at Siracusa.

The rivers flowing to the south coast are long, wandering and slow-flowing; the main ones are the Disueri (or Gela), Salso,

Platani and Belice. Many Sicilian rivers have alternative names or, more commonly, different names for different reaches. The Salso or Imera Meridionale is, at 112km, the longest river in Sicily, but the area of its drainage basin, 2,002sq km, is only half that of the Simeto, and its summer flow is negligible.

There are very few lakes. The most famous is L Pergusa near Enna (also called the Lake of Blood because of the reddish colour of the water—caused by the presence of certain organisms). The lake, which lies at an altitude of 667m, has an area of 2sq km and a depth of only 4m. With its panoramic encircling road (used for frequent motor races), its tourist village, water skiing, flower-bedecked green slopes and eucalyptus woods, L Pergusa is one of the most pleasant but most commercialised places in the interior.

Apart from very small and mostly ephemeral patches of inland water, the rest of the natural lakes are coastal. The Biviere or L Lentini, now drained and cultivated, was once the island's largest lake, and there are stretches of water, varying in size according to season, along the south coast near Gela and Scoglitti. Two lakes—Pantano Grande and Piccolo—at the north-east tip of Sicily, although shut in behind a shingle bar, have been linked to the sea since the 1908 earthquake and are now flourishing oyster beds. The topographical map reveals several quite large reservoirs dammed for irrigation water and hydro-electric power—L di Disueri near Gela, L Arancio near Sambuca, L Trinità near Castelvetrano and L Piana degli Albanesi near the town of the same name—as well as numerous smaller earth-dammed lakes.

CLIMATE

The island's climate is classically Mediterranean in character. The seasonal regime is very marked, hot dry summers contrasting with cool, rainy winters. In terms of mean annual temperatures, most of the climate stations record figures of

15–18° C. Only the highest villages record somewhat lower averages (Petralia Sottana at 1,000m, 14° C; Floresta at 1,275m, 11° C), although the higher uninhabited elevations are much colder again, down to an annual average of 0° C on the summit of Etna. The warmest places in terms of mean annual temperatures are on or near the coasts; Cefalù, Milazzo, Ragusa and Mazara del Vallo all have 19° C.

More meaningful, however, is a comparison between the contrasting summer and winter temperatures. The mean annual range is lowest on the coast, due to the equalising influence of the sea (14° C at Marsala on the west coast and 15° C at Acireale on the east) and highest inland where effects of altitude and continentality prevail; Caltanissetta has a range of 19° C and Nicosia 20° C. Summer temperatures are fairly uniform over most of the island, averaging about 24–27° C for the means of the hottest months (July and August). The hottest places are in the south-east; Ragusa (Iblei) and Raddusa (Catania Plain) both have mean August temperatures of 29° C. Most places are capable of reaching 35° C frequently during the summer, and occasionally the thermometer tops 40° C. These very hot conditions usually apply when the *scirocco* blows, bringing hot, dusty, and often humid air from the Sahara, making life very enervating, especially along the south coast. Mean temperatures for January and February are above 10° C only on the coasts. Inland they fall rapidly with increasing altitude: Nicosia at 800m, 5° C; Etna Observatory at 2,950m, −6° C.

The greater part of the island receives a mean annual rainfall of 600–700mm, although great variation occurs from year to year. The figure rises above 1,000mm only along the northern mountain chain and on the higher slopes of Etna. Rainfall of below 500mm occurs along most of the south coast from Trapani to Siracusa, and in the Plain of Catania. The lowest (300–400mm) is received by the Pachino peninsula and the islands south of Sicily (Pantellaria, Lampedusa and Linosa).

Most rain comes in winter, borne by humid winds from the west and north-west. Especially in late autumn, the character of the rainfall is extremely violent. Summer rainfall is uniformly low at about 20–50mm (around 5 per cent of the annual total). In fact many summers are completely rainless, which means a constant fight against drought.

VEGETATION AND ANIMAL LIFE

With over 90 per cent of Sicily's area under productive use—cultivation and pasture—very little of the original vegetation is left. The present woodland cover, 63,000ha, is very unevenly distributed, well over half of it, chiefly in the form of oak and elm, clothing the mountains of Messina province. Only Catania (10,000ha, mostly on Etna) and Palermo (7,000ha, chiefly in the Forest of Ficuzza) of the other provinces have significant forest areas. Agrigento, Ragusa, Siracusa and Trapani have only 2,000ha between them.

At low elevations, the few areas that remain uncultivated are under scrub vegetation, either maquis or garrigue. Maquis is formed by an exuberant variety of highly scented Mediterranean shrubbery, including oleander, lentisk, asphodel, tamarisk, myrtle, tree heather and numerous other aromatic plants. Where it is particularly luxuriant, as along the lower slopes of the northern mountains, maquis vegetation can reach 2–3m in height and include various dwarf trees, olives, carobs, Aleppo pines and even holm and cork oaks. The maquis mostly results from secondary colonisation of former forest land or of land passing out of cultivation. Towards the southern part of the island, however, the dense maquis degenerates into more drought-resistant garrigue. Garrigue species are more spiny and cactoid, adapted to withstand the long, hot, dormant summer. They include cistus, heathers, spiny broom, wormwood, a few junipers and a very dry spiky grass called *stipa*. Along the dry sandy shores of the south coast, palm trees give the scene a distinctly African aspect. Everywhere both maquis and garrigue are infiltrated by agave and prickly pear cactus; introduced from Latin America 300 years ago, they are now so widespread as to form an essential part of the landscape.

Maquis and garrigue occupy areas generally below 400m, though the former can be found up to 700–800m, the upper limit of the wild olive. Cultivation in general tends to fall off above this elevation, being replaced by pasture and the remaining areas of woodland. Above about 750m, extending up to 1,400m, such woodland as is found is oak, often intermixed with elm, ash and maple. Large sweet-chestnut woods occur, at elevations ranging from 300 to 1,700m, under the Rocca Busambra (Forest of Ficuzza) in Palermo province, along the Peloritani and around Etna. Above 1,400m trees more accustomed to temperate climates are found. There are a few glorious beech-woods in the Madonie and Nebrodi Mountains and on Etna, also the larch and various conifers. A dwarf form of birch occurs as high as 2,340m on Etna. Alpine vegetation is limited to the great volcano, with juniper scrub and degraded volcanic ash vegetation topping the 3,000m mark.

Animal and bird life have much in common with those of southern Italy, which is to be expected, but the variety is much poorer in Sicily. The main wild animals to be found in the countryside are the wolf, fox, hare, rabbit, weasel, porcupine, hedgehog, and various varieties of mice, snakes and lizards. Bats and wild swans are notable amongst the larger avifauna. Some birds, such as the ringed plover, and the black and griffon vultures, are shared only with Sardinia; the pratincole and the bearded vulture are shared with Spain and the Balkans; and the black wheatear with Spain and Sardinia. Many migratory birds use the island as a staging post on their annual movements between Africa and Europe.

REGIONAL LANDSCAPES

Within the neat triangular outline of Sicily a number of fairly distinct regions can be recognised. The one true mountain range, made up of the Peloritani, Nebrodi and Madonie groups, contains the most beautiful and dramatic of the island's scenery. Orange groves form a continuous belt along the coast between Messina and Taormina, succeeded inland by vines and olives grown on terraces up to about 500m, although the upper flights are being abandoned to the scrub and pasture which extend to the mountain summits. Because of the rugged nature of the terrain, settlement and roads are confined to below about 400m. The villages lie up the mountain flanks a few kilometres from the coast, reached by steep winding roads that go no farther. No road crosses the Peloritani from one coast to the other, only the main road behind Messina at the end of the range. These interior villages of the Peloritani with their subsistence pasture-based economies, remote from the good land, the road and railway and the beaches of the coast, are gradually declining. Many lost a quarter of their populations during 1951–61; meanwhile the coastal *marina* settlements, strung out along the main road in a continuous ribbon development in places, especially east of Milazzo, grow rapidly. Farther west, where the mountains broaden to massifs and plateaux, a true upland economy is evident, with several villages above 1,000m (Floresta, S Domenica Vittoria, Cesarò, Capizzi, Geraci Siculo) and many more just below. Although the Nebrodi and Madonie are nearly twice as high as the Peloritani, a number of roads make the north-south crossing, pursuing tortuous, scenic and lonely routes through the mountains. The highest of these routes, between Cesarò and S Fratello, reaches 1,524m in the Portella Femmina Morta.

Crossing the northern mountains the traveller reaches an entirely different landscape. The northern slopes of the Nebrodi and Madonie are steep, almost cliffed in places, but the southern gradient trends more gently down to the plateaux of central Sicily, the vast expanses of bare, desolate cereal country that cover much of the interior. For Lampedusa, author of *The Leopard*, this is the 'real' Sicily,

> . . . the one compared to which baroque towns and olive groves are mere trifles: aridly undulating to the horizon in hillock after hillock, comfortless and irrational, with no lines that the mind could grasp, conceived apparently in a delirious moment of creation; a sea suddenly petrified at the instant when a change of wind had flung the waves into a frenzy.

Certainly the interior, protected by the northern mountains from rain-bearing winds and open to the penetration of the hot dessicating Saharan southerlies, has an arid steppe-like appearance; a tormented mass of dry clay hills devoid of trees and farms, burnt to a sickly yellow in summer, green only for a short spring. There is a haunting quality about central Sicily, a sense of timelessness. Grey villages on distant hilltops fade into the landscape as if they had been carved from the rock itself, as indeed parts of some of them have. Agira, Gangi and Prizzi cover complete mountains with their chaotic jumble of buildings. Other places, like Marineo and Corleone, cluster on ledges overhung by precipitous crags.

The poverty of the interior is easily recognised in the rather squalid appearance of most of the villages. Small, box-like hovels with flat or sloping roofs built often of unfinished cement blocks are set back-to-back amongst narrow, cobbled or mud alleys. Apart from a little modern speculative building and some small government rehousing projects, the character of these settlements changes little. Few tourists visit such places; if they do they are likely to be put off by the unashamed, staring curiosity of the inhabitants. The majority of interior settlements have populations of over 5,000 and are located at altitudes of 500–700m (higher towards the north and towards the Erei Mountains). Dispersed farms, apart from the occasional *masseria*, or estate headquarters, are almost entirely lacking.

The life and economy of central Sicily has centuries of feudal tradition behind it. The feudal structure was well established by Norman times, but most interior villages were created by feudal overlords for their agricultural labourers when the cereal boom of the fifteenth to early eighteenth centuries led to a massive extension of this monoculture over the clay lands. Burgio (fifteenth century), Vallelunga Pratameno (sixteenth), Ravanusa (seventeenth) and Villalba (eighteenth) are all foundations of this period, and there are over a hundred more like them. When viewed from afar, the massive outline of the feudal castle can be seen at one end of the village; at the other the sharper but less imposing silhouette of the baroque church, and in between, indistinguishable one from the other in their multitude, the humble dwellings of the peasants. This simple, symbolic picture of feudal Sicily is repeated dozens of times throughout the island.

Road signs on many interior roads warn the traveller of *frane*. These landslips occur when the clay becomes so saturated with water during a heavy rainfall that it virtually becomes a mud-flow. *Frane* are a constant threat to agriculture, settlement and communications in central Sicily. The main Palermo–Catania railway is blocked by a *frana* nearly every year between Villa-rosa and Enna, and many roads are likewise interrupted. Crops may be smothered or washed away, and buildings constructed on the clay are liable to cracks, subsidence and collapse.

Western Sicily is a diverse landscape of undulating plains interrupted by isolated limestone mountains and headlands. Enormous vineyards smother the flatter plains behind Trapani, Marsala and Mazara del Vallo, stretching as far as the eye can see and relieved only by the scatter of small white hamlets in which the viticulturalists live. To the north, bold limestone promontories define a series of broad bays. The easternmost of these bays provides the splendid setting for Palermo and its fertile hinterland. The view from the enormous rock lump of M Pellegrino is one of the most beautiful in Sicily. To the left lies the throbbing capital city set round its incomparable bay, with the purple Madonie in the distance. To the right are the lighter shades of the steep Castellaccio and Cuccio ranges. Between them stretches the brief expanse of plain, known as the Conca d'Oro (Shell of Gold) since the sixteenth century, that surrounds the city, stretching from Mondello round in an arc to Bagheria. Viewed from above, the Conca d'Oro's dominant colour is the dark metallic green of the citrus groves, punctuated by a dense scatter of small, white cubic houses. Powerful springs issuing from the base of the limestone mountains provide plentiful irrigation water for the groves of oranges and lemons which extend inland up the Oreto and Eleutero valleys.

Eastern Sicily south of the Peloritani is made up of three well-defined and contrasting regions. M Etna, separated from the Peloritani by the Alcantara valley and from the grainlands of central Sicily by the Simeto, is a unique feature (see Chapter 11). The Catania Plain is one of Sicily's newest landscapes, following a systematic reclamation policy based on malaria eradication, flood control, drainage, irrigation, roads, new farms and villages. Two dams on Simeto tributaries enable storage of winter floodwaters for summer irrigation, supplied to the plain by an extensive network of canals and concrete channels. 40,000ha are now under irrigated crops of cotton, forage for dairy cows, and citrus fruits. The Plain of Catania is about to replay its classical role as one of the richest farming areas in the island.

In the extreme south-eastern corner of Sicily is the prosperous Iblean region. Here agriculture is well-developed and specialised, in spite of the island's lowest rainfall—below 400mm on the coasts—and the landscape is further diversified by the growth of modern industrial complexes at Ragusa, Augusta and Siracusa. During Ancient Greek times Siracusa was one of the largest and richest cities in the Mediterranean. Papyrus, imported by the Greeks from the Nile Valley, still grows today along the banks of the Anapo river. Although almost the entire region was devastated by an earthquake in 1693, it is a measure of its people's prosperity and enterprise that the new cities that rose to replace the old were finely laid out in a lavish and beautiful baroque. Most of the smaller agricultural towns were also planned afresh, often on startling geometrical designs as at Avola and Grammichele. The refinement and gentleness of the people of Siracusa and other towns in these parts—characteristics often exaggeratedly attributed to the people's Greek heritage—are unique in Sicily.

There is considerable contrast in land use and scenery between the higher Iblei plateaux around M Lauro and those areas with more richly weathered soils lower down, although everywhere the fields are divided by dry-stone walls that make use of the surface litter of limestone and basalt boulders. The high tablelands are still under a traditional cereal-pastoral regime, and the villages—Buccheri, Buscemi, and Vizzini (birthplace of Verga)—are noticeably poorer. Buccheri, 820m above sea level, was once noted for its trade in ice and snow, stored in caves in the hills round about; it is now beginning to be used as a summer resort by people of the coast. The *cave*, steep sided ravines cut in the limestone, lead down to the more fertile lowlands. They are mostly too narrow and tortuous to serve as modern routeways, but were much used in ancient times for habitation, refuge and burial chambers. The Pantalica necropolis of 5,000 excavated caves dating from the Siculan period (twelfth to eighth centuries BC) is to be found near Sortino in the Anapo valley, and other prehistoric caves exist in the famous Cava d'Ispica east of Modica. Many peasant homes today, as well as several churches, are excavated out of the rock.

The lower, peripheral parts of the Iblei have been transformed since the eighteenth century by arduous peasant labour from former estate range land into vineyards, fruit orchards and vegetable gardens. Local specialisation of crops is well marked: citrus orchards in the north around Carlentini, Francofonte and Scordia; almonds and carobs around Noto and Avola; viti-

Page 35 (*above*) The attractive coastline below Taormina; Capo Sant'Andrea and the Isola Bella; (*below*) view of Trapani, a provincial capital, from the slopes of Mount Eryx

Page 36 (above) Castellammare del Golfo, a fishing port on the north coast of western Sicily, notorious for delinquency and its involvement with the Mafia; (below) Ustica, a peaceful island, formerly a place of banishment for criminals

culture in the Pachino peninsula; interculture of orchards and horticulture between Ispica and S Croce Camerina, and splendid vineyards again around and to the north of Vittoria. Most of the farmers live in large agro-towns of 30,000–50,000 inhabitants, commuting outwards to their fields by car, scooter, bicycle and occasionally still by donkey and cart.

3 THE ARCHAEOLOGICAL AND ARCHITECTURAL HERITAGE

THE BEGINNING

EARLY man arrived in Sicily by sea, perhaps before 20,000 BC, at the end of the Würm glaciation. The earliest remains, dating from the Upper Palaeolithic, are distributed along the northern, western and south-eastern coasts. Upper Palaeolithic man dwelt in caves; the two most famous, with beautiful cave paintings, are on the island of Levanzo off Trapani (Grotta della Cala dei Genovesi) and on M Pellegrino

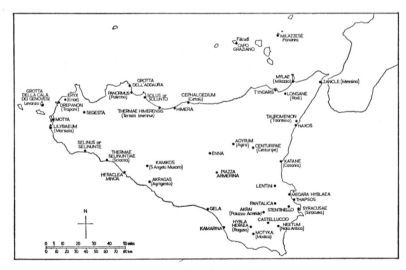

D   The main archaeological sites

near Palermo (Grotta dell'Addaura). A radio-carbon date of about 10,000 BC has been obtained for Levanzo, but the chronology of these earliest inhabitants is very obscure.

The Paleaolithic tradition lasted until the fourth millennium BC, when new people brought the Neolithic culture from the eastern Mediterranean. The earliest Sicilian Neolithic is known as the Stentinello culture, after the village near Siracusa where it was first identified. These people were farmers: they built themselves hut villages, reared animals and cultivated the land. Stentinello pottery, akin to that of northern Greece, decorated with impressions of finger-nails, shells and birds' bones, is the earliest known in Sicily. More advanced Neolithic peoples prospered on the Eolian Islands, trading the obsidian in which the islands abound.

By about 3000 BC new immigrants brought metal-working to Sicily; they came, again, from the eastern Mediterranean and the Aegean. The Copper Age is a time of great archaeological complexity in Sicily, a period of rapid transformation in which each locality had its own characteristics and changing traditions. New advances in sea travel put Sicily more closely in touch with surrounding land masses, and the island's civilisation also received influences from Malta, Sardinia, France, and particularly the Iberian peninsula, whence came the Beaker Culture. Copper Age civilisation was especially dense around Palermo where a distinct subculture, the Conca d'Oro, is recognised. Copper Age people buried their dead in rock-cut tombs (called *tombe a forno* because of their similarity to Sicilian peasant ovens), a custom ideally suited to the predominant limestone geology and one which was to remain for many centuries, surviving until the complete hellenisation of Sicily in the fifth century BC.

Really widespread metal-working in Sicily came with the Bronze Age in the early second millennium BC, a transition which occurred without any cultural upheaval or break in the archaeological record. The Bronze Age was particularly pros-

39

perous in the Eolian Islands, with the development of the Capo Graziano culture (on Filicudi island: early Bronze Age) and the Milazzese culture (on Panarea: middle Bronze Age). In mainland Sicily the corresponding type-cultures are the Castelluccio (between Ragusa and Noto: large group of rock-cut tombs) for the early Bronze Age and the Thapsos (between Siracusa and Augusta) for the middle; though for both periods the number of sites is large, covering most parts of the island. Little groups of rock-cut tombs are present throughout the limestone area of eastern Sicily, as well as elsewhere, but there is nothing to match the several hundred tombs at Castelluccio, some of which have spirally decorated portal slabs—the only examples of Sicilian prehistoric stone carving.

The prosperous civilisation of the early and middle Bronze Age periods came to an abrupt end about 1250 BC. During the late Bronze Age, new invaders—the Sicels and the Ausonians—came from mainland Italy. Under constant threat of invasion, civilisation shifted inland from exposed coastal sites like Thapsos. New, much larger, settlements were set up in inaccessible hill regions, of which the chief visible remnant is the huge Pantalica necropolis near Sortino. With its large area and fine defensive site, Pantalica was undoubtedly the most important pre-Greek centre in Sicily. Other late Bronze Age sites were at Cassibile, where a mountainside is riddled with some 2,000 tombs, Modica, Ragusa, Caltagirone and Noto Antica.

By about 1000 BC, Phoenicians began trading objects from all parts of the Mediterranean with Sicily. They probably brought iron and certainly ousted the earlier domination of Mycenaean goods. Sicily at this time, immediately prior to the Greek colonisation, was dominated by three native tribal groupings: the Sicels in the east, the Sicans in the west and the Elymians in the far north-west. Many present-day hill-top settlements in Sicily were once Sicel strongholds, and Elymian centres existed at Erice and Segesta. Much less is known about the Sicans. Diodorus says they once lived in the east of the island, but were driven west by eruptions of Etna, to be replaced by the Sicels. Only one Sican town is identifiable today with any certainty: this is Kamikos, the modern S Angelo Muxaro, where there is an outstanding series of chamber tombs.

CLASSICAL SICILY: GREECE, ROME AND CARTHAGE

Early in the first millennium BC, Sicily was already being colonised by the Phoenicians in the west and the Greeks in the east. The Greek annexation of the island was rapid, intense and well organised, especially on the Ionian coast. The first colony was the relatively unimportant one of Naxos, founded in 734 BC on the lava peninsula of Capo Schisò near Taormina (then the Sicel settlement of Tauromenion) by Greeks from Chalcis and the island of Naxos (hence the colony's name). The next ten years saw two larger colonies founded by the Naxians: Leontinoi (Lentini) and Katane (Catania); as well as Syracusa by Corinthians; Megara Hyblaea by men from Megara; and Zancle (Messina) by a joint effort of Cumae and Chalcis. In 689 BC the first colonising wave from Greece was completed with the foundation of Gela by a combined Cretan-Rhodian expedition, but already the earlier Sicilian colonies had started establishing their own daughter settlements. Zancle founded Mylae (Milazzo) around 715 BC and Himera in 648 BC, both on the north coast. From the south-east Syracusa extended dominion over much of the interior and south coast, occupying the Sicel towns of Akrai (Palazzo Acreide) and Kasmenai (M Casale), and founding Kamarina. The Megarans founded Selinus, the most westerly Greek town in Sicily, in either 650 or 628 BC. Finally, Gela founded Akragas (Agrigento) soon after 600 BC. Within 135 years the colonisation of much of coastal and eastern Sicily was complete, although it was another century or more before much of the interior as far as Enna (the Sicel 'Henna') and Segesta (the Elymian 'Egesta') was hellenised. The Greek tongue became widespread, and survived in fact well into the

41

succeeding Roman period. The Greek colonies rapidly developed into powerful entities independent of the motherland, and witnessed a period of great cultural growth. During the 500 years of Greek civilisation, these cities became centres of beauty and learning, great maritime powers, surrounded by fertile and well-tilled land. The Greeks introduced the vine, the olive, the fig and several other plants to the island. Archimedes, Aeschylus, Diodorus and Theocritus were all Sicilian Greeks. The march of cultural achievement was, however, frequently interrupted by warfare, either with the Carthaginians or between the Greek cities themselves. The men who rose to power in these cities, men often of humble origin who were able to champion popular discontent, were known as tyrants. Examples are Theron of Akragas, Hippocrates of Gela, Timoleon and Dion of Syracusa; there were numerous others. Gelon of Syracusa was probably the most important individual in Europe in the fifth century BC.

The legacy of Greece in Sicily is tremendous. The most spectacular temples are at Agrigento. In 480 BC Theron of Akragas and Gelon of Syracusa combined to inflict crushing defeat on the Carthaginians. So much booty and so many slaves were taken that Theron was able to embark upon a colossal campaign of temple-building. The Temple of Concord is one of the most perfectly preserved in the Ancient Greek world and the unfinished Temple of Zeus would have been its largest existing structure: an earthquake brought it down in antiquity and much of its stone went to build Porto Empedocle harbour in the eighteenth century. Many consider the unfinished temple at Segesta to be the finest archaeological monument in Sicily. Aloft on a great platform amongst the summits of interior western Sicily, open to the sun, the wind and the rain and speckled by drifting cloud shadows, its situation is unique and its symmetry perfect. There are extensive remains too at Selinus or Selinunte, once a thriving south coast seaport; they are left much as they were when destroyed, first by Hannibal and the Carthaginians in 409 BC, and again in about 250 BC. But the largest Greek city in Sicily, indeed in the whole of Europe at the time, was Syracusa, the home of Archimedes and of the most powerful rulers in the island. Its fine Greek theatre is still used to perform the plays first heard there 2,300 years ago, and the Temple of Athena is incorporated into the city's cathedral.

The Roman conquest began in 264 BC and, after the victory of Rome in the Second Punic War (215 BC), the whole island was occupied by 210 BC. Throughout this third century there had been much destruction of Greek cities like Akragas and Selinunte and of Carthaginian strongholds such as Lilybaeum and Panormus. Under the Roman Republic, Sicily was exploited for everything it had to offer and rapidly lost much of its prosperity. The 'Granary of Rome'—the island's prime function was to feed the Roman army—was laid out in huge estates, called latifundia, cultivated by slaves. Conditions were so harsh that two Slave Wars broke out around 135–132 and 104–101 BC. In the first century BC, Cicero went to Sicily and attributed its decline to the negligent behaviour of the praetor Verres. With the advent of the empire, however, and the passing of Verres, Sicily appears to have recovered a measure of prosperity. The archaeological evidence speaks of a well-populated countryside with clusters of villages, hamlets and villas in most parts of the island. Imperial Rome left behind considerable architectural remains at Taormina, Catania, Siracusa, Solunto, Termini Imerese and Palermo. The most singular piece of Roman Sicily is the much later (AD second to third century) villa at Casale (near Piazza Armerina), a place famed for its splendid mosaic pavements and possibly owned by the Emperor Maximian. In seven centuries of Roman occupation the Sicilian-Greek vernacular became inalienably Latin, and, in spite of a revival of Byzantine Greek and later contributions of Arabic to place-names and dialect, has remained so ever since.

Christianity came early to Sicily. St Paul visited Siracusa en route for Rome in the second century AD, the same century as the earliest, tentative archaeological and literary evidence. Jewish communities existed at least by the fourth century. Pagan temples everywhere were destroyed or converted to Christian churches, and catacombs and cemeteries multiplied; those of Siracusa being more extensive even than the catacombs of Rome. Sicily has been called the classic land of early Christian funerary architecture. Rustic chapels, called *cube*, and troglodytic sanctuaries have been discovered all over the island, though few are anything like complete, having suffered at the hands of the Barbarians and the Arabs.

ARABS AND NORMANS

The Vandals and the Ostrogoths raided Sicily in the fifth century, and less than a century later the island was swiftly incorporated into the Byzantine Empire on the order of the Emperor Justinian. Much trouble was engendered by the different views of the churches of the Eastern and Western Roman Empires, a conflict further embittered by the transference of the Byzantine capital from Constantinople to Siracusa in 683. Four popes between 678 and 701 were Sicilian. Siracusa remained the capital for five years until Emperor Constans was assassinated in his bath by his chamberlain wielding a soap-dish. Details of the 300 years of Byzantine rule are, nevertheless, very few, and hardly any monuments remain from the sixth to the ninth centuries.

Sicily had already been threatened by piratical Arab raids in 652 and 669; during the eighth century these became increasingly frequent. In 827 an élite army of 10,000 Berbers, Arabians and Spanish moslems landed at Mazara del Vallo and commenced the Islamic conquest of Sicily, a campaign which lasted half a century, bringing widespread destruction, famine and massacre. Palermo fell in 831, Messina in 843, Cefalù in

858, Enna in 859 and the key city of Siracusa in 878. For 1,500 years Siracusa had been the first city of Sicily, probably of Europe and the Ancient World; it was now compelled to play second fiddle to Palermo. The Saracens, who crossed from the area today called Tunisia, set up their capital at Palermo, and the island began to flourish anew. It became an independent province and the geographical centre of an economic empire that stretched from one end of the Mediterranean to the other, and beyond. Agriculture developed dramatically with the introduction of irrigation and several new crops—sugar cane, cotton, the mulberry, date-palm, carob and lemon. The Arabs improved fishing techniques, and produced silver, lead, mercury, sulphur, alum and rock-salt. Palermo became a great cultural centre famed for its 300 mosques and its progressive cosmopolitan population of Greeks, Slavs, Jews, Persians and Negroes.

When the Byzantines under Maniakes, together with a contingent of Normans, attacked the eastern part of the island in 1038, Arab Sicily was already in decline. The Normans, led by the brothers Robert and Roger de Hauteville, professional soldiers with many years campaigning in southern Italy behind them, returned to conquer Sicily on their own, starting with Messina in 1061 and ending with the last moslem stronghold at Noto in 1091. There were many bloody battles, none more so than the desperate fight for the big prize of Palermo in 1071. Although the institution of a benevolent kind of feudalism brought a number of Norman, French and Lombard landowners in from the north (evidenced by the French and north Italian names of Sicilian villages founded between 1090 and 1250), the Norman conquest of Sicily was not a settlement en masse like that of the Arabs. Finding that they came into contact with a genuinely superior civilisation, the Normans gave the Arab and Greek populations full reign to develop science, art, poetry and architecture, contributing themselves a useful degree of organisational vigour and efficiency. Count Roger, and later Roger II, first King of Sicily, ruled with a degree of religious, linguistic and cultural tolerance hitherto unknown. The mixture of the best from the Arab, Byzantine and north European cultures made the period brilliantly successful and combined perfectly to create the distinct Sicilian Norman style of architecture, seen at its best in the cathedrals of Monreale and Cefalù. In the royal palace in Palermo, in the city's cathedral (much altered in subsequent periods) and in several of its churches (notably S Giovanni degli Eremiti and S Maria dell'Ammariglio), Norman heaviness is everywhere tempered by Arab domes and cloisters and Byzantine mosaics. The Normans also built castles, at Mazara, Palermo, Monreale, Paternò and elsewhere.

SPAIN IN SICILY

Eventually the brilliance of Norman Sicily declined and was lost. The island came under Swabian rule for a time, due to the marriage in 1194 of Constance, sister of William the Bad (one of the later Norman kings), to the German emperor Henry IV of Hohenstaufen. Henry's son, Frederick I of Sicily and II of Hohenstaufen, dubbed *stupor mundi*, the 'wonder of the world', was an able ruler, more cultivated and intellectual in fact than any of his Norman predecessors, but with a hint of ruthlessness and lust that alienated him from Sicilians. To him are owed many of the finest castles, such as the Ursino in Catania and the Castello Maniace in Siracusa. He also refounded Gela, abandoned since the close of the classical era. The short Swabian period came to an end in 1268, to be followed by an even shorter interval under the Angevins, when the pope invited Charles of Anjou to be king of Sicily. Angevin rule ended in 1282 with the famous revolt of the Sicilian Vespers, which threw out the oppressive French.

There followed a long association with Spain, first as ally to oust the French, and then, after the Treaty of Caltabellotta in

1302, as an independent kingdom under the House of Aragon. Frederick II of Sicily (1296–1337) proved to be the island's fourth wise medieval king (after Roger II, William the Good and Frederick I), successfully marrying Catalan and Latin interests into a united front against the Angevins, the Guelphs and the Papacy. This period is distinguished by Gothic-Renaissance architecture (also called Chiaramonte, after the prominent French Clermont family in Sicily) which reached noteworthy proportions in the Chiaramonte and Sclafani palaces in Palermo; the Santo Spirito convent in Agrigento; and the Montalto and Bellomo palaces in Siracusa. Also of this period are the small decorated *palazzi* of Taormina, built of contrasting blocks of lava, pumice and limestone. With the death in 1377 of Frederick III, Sicily collapsed into anarchy, with one Aragonese prince after another claiming the throne. In 1409 the island lost its autonomy and became a Spanish dependency to be ruled by a succession of seventy-eight viceroys over the next 300 years.

Spanish rule on the whole did not benefit Sicily, which sank into obscurity and decay. However, Spanish customs and language filtered into the island and, in all, a great deal was absorbed during those three centuries. Quantitatively the Spaniards raised more historic buildings in Sicily than any other people, although there is little that can genuinely be termed Spanish baroque; the best work was done by native architects who had trained in Rome. The fifteenth and sixteenth centuries are responsible for Carnclivari's fine Aiutamicristo and Abbatelli palaces in Palermo and for the exquisite, many-marbled church of Santa Catarina, also in the capital. The seventeenth and early eighteenth centuries, however, gave the majority of towns their prevalently baroque character. Hundreds of baroque churches and palaces all over the island testify to the building energy of the later Spanish viceroys. The Dukes of Osuna, Maqueda and Vigliena (the last-named built the Quattro Canti in Palermo) were indefatigable embellishers of towns. Much minor architecture, such as balconies, shrines, public fountains and monuments, also dates from the exuberant Spanish baroque period. Another notable feature is the stucco work of Serpotta, seen at its best in the delightful rococo oratories of Palermo. Siracusa, Catania, Modica, Ragusa and several other towns rebuilt after the 1693 earthquake are full of striking, early eighteenth-century palaces and churches; the supreme example is Noto, planned completely anew, where the wonderfully and grotesquely ornate, honey-coloured architecture survives barely altered to this day.

SICILY: BOURBON AND ITALIAN

The Treaty with Utrecht, which concluded in 1713 the long War of Spanish Succession, gave Sicily to Savoy and Sardinia to Austria; by the Treaty of The Hague (1720) the islands were exchanged and Sicily passed to Austria. In 1734, the islanders entered into the long Bourbon domination, when the Spaniards were welcomed as a desperate alternative to the detested Austrians. When the new king of Sicily, Charles III, was promoted to the throne of Spain in 1759, the rest of Europe would not let him keep Sicily and Naples as well, so these two kingdoms passed to his son, who became Ferdinand I of Sicily and IV of Naples.

The early years of Bourbon rule were quite progressive, but social extravagance reached almost unprecedented levels in the capital, bringing ruin to many families as is shown by the half-finished palaces and baroque façades surviving today. Palermo had some of the most splendid theatres in Europe long before it had a reasonable hospital. A great degree of poverty still existed in the countryside, and banditry flourished as never before. Sicily at this time was linked with Naples (ie the whole of mainland southern Italy) in the dual Kingdom of the Two Sicilies. The seat of the Bourbon government was Naples, and the island, remote from the administrative centre supposedly governing it, suffered increasingly during the second half of the eighteenth century. After the bad harvest of 1773 and the Palermo revolt of the same year, Viceroys Caracciolo and Caramanico introduced some well intentioned reforms in the 1780s which weakened feudalism considerably, but after 1789 and the French Revolution the king and his reactionary advisors halted the process.

It was during the long reign of Ferdinand I, who left most of the cares of governing the island to his unscrupulous wife Maria Carolina of Austria, that Napoleon invaded Naples. Britain needed Sicily as a strategic base for the war against Bonaparte, and occupied the island between 1806 and 1815 in return for an annual subsidy and 10,000 men to defend Messina and Augusta. Lord Bentinck, the British plenipotentiary, exercised great influence on internal affairs, securing the withdrawal of the meddlesome Maria Carolina, abolishing feudalism, and reforming the Sicilian parliament along British lines in 1812. More than 17,000 British soldiers were in occupation and brought new economic life to the island. In 1816 Austrian intervention and some crafty work by Ferdinand (restyling himself Ferdinand I of the United Kingdom of the Two Sicilies) resulted in the demise of British influence and the removal once more of the monarchy to Naples where it resumed authoritarian rule.

The period 1820–60 was one of revolts and new ideas, for these were the years of the Risorgimento, leading up to Sicily's unification with Italy. There were Sicilian revolts in 1820, 1831, 1837 (linked to a cholera plague) and, of course, 1848. An abortive uprising in Palermo early in 1860 stirred the whole island. Francesco Crispi, a lawyer and disciple of Mazzini and later to become Italian prime minister, appealed to Garibaldi who immediately landed at Marsala with his famous red-shirted Thousand. By a mixture of brilliance, luck and bluffing, Garibaldi defeated 3,000 Bourbonist troops at Catalafimi and then successfully occupied Palermo. Another desperate battle against the Bourbons at Milazzo was won by Garibaldi. In the late summer of 1860 he crossed to Calabria, taking Reggio, and proceeded up the Italian peninsula, making Italian unity inevitable. In the autumn Sicily voted its adherence to the new kingdom of Italy, though Messina, so often the first or last to fall, did not surrender till 1861.

Architecturally the nineteenth century produced little of note in Sicily. In the present century, the fascist regime constructed many buildings in the grand style (mostly, like the enormous post office in Palermo, neo-classical or neo-Renaissance), but few can be deemed aesthetically pleasing. Fascism did achieve a great deal in road, railway and aqueduct building, and the interwar period also saw the new tendency of isolated farmsteads dotting the interior estate lands, but few of these cottages were ever lived in and most are now in ruin.

Much of the post-war construction boom, especially round the coasts and in the larger towns, takes the form of characterless blocks of flats or offices, and exhibits a total lack of planning or concern for preserving the architectural environment. Recent speculative building has ruined stretches of coastline and the suburban approaches to many fine historic cities, in particular Trapani. Everywhere lack of social planning is evident: no public parks or open spaces are left when the speculator is allowed to build over every bit of urban and suburban land. Equally deplorable is the lack of concern, and no doubt of finance, to preserve the many fine buildings, some of them priceless architectural treasures. Sicily may be almost over-rich in legacies from the past but, once lost, this wealth can never be recovered.

4   THE SICILIAN WAY OF LIFE

MANY visitors from northern Europe find the islanders'
way of life raucous and noisy for Sicilians are extremely gregarious—as they have to be, crowded
together as they are—and fond of clamour. Much of their life
takes place out of doors, as a glimpse down any alley or back
street reveals. Tables, chairs and household goods are placed
outside the door, and all manner of household activities enliven
the scene; eating, washing, sewing, repairing or just gossiping.
Children and livestock of indeterminate ownership swarm
everywhere, and the noise from transistor radios, revving
scooters, infants and *mammas* is cacophonous.

Life revolves round the family, which in Sicily means putting
the family before all else. It also means that the individual finds
refuge in the family against the injustices and cruelties of the
outside world; that suspicion, scepticism and apathy are rife;
and that any co-operative action is extraordinarily difficult to
stimulate because once outside the family everyone is mutually
competitive and thus open to manipulation from above—by
priests, mayors, the police, the Mafia and the local political
party bosses. Poverty, ignorance, illiteracy and family bonds
thus combine in a conspiracy against progress. Wherever
modernisation has taken place it has come about not from
within, but exogenously through radio, television, military
service and emigration.

The family is an immensely strong and rigid social unit.
Only in the more modern eastern towns, where industrialisation
has brought with it the morals and values of northern Italy, is

51

the family losing its strength. In Sicily, four or five generations may be living under the same roof. Old people are automatically taken care of within the family and the opinions of aged grandparents are respected and valued. Kinship networks are very strong, and often very extensive, due to the large number of children and the practice of marrying distant relatives. Inter-family feuds used to reach vendetta proportions, involving dozens of people, especially when the Mafia was implicated, and reprisals in the form of murder are still common, especially where 'honour' is at stake. If the honour of a man's sister or daughter is besmirched (and this by no means involves seduction), family honour is only restored when the aggressor is either killed or married to the girl.

Within the family, men and women lead very different lives from each other. The man, as breadwinner and head of the family, has complete mastery over his wife, enjoying many privileges which she cannot aspire to. He has freedom to do what he likes. Sicily is a man's club. The women stay at home. The bars are exclusively male territory. The evening *passeggiata*, the ritual strolling up and down the *corso* common to most Mediterranean countries, is very much male-dominated. In some villages in western Sicily few women are allowed even to do the shopping or collect water from the public fountain; such seclusion is said to be a relic of the Islamic occupation. Young girls, after puberty, are rarely seen out of the house, and if they attend Mass on Sundays, for example, are closely chaperoned. Widows usually remain in mourning for their husbands for the rest of their lives and it is not uncommon to find an old woman who has worn black for maybe fifty years, following a succession of family bereavements.

Female employment in factories and offices is more or less limited to the east coast cities and to Palermo. Only a tenth of industrial workers are female, compared to a third in northern Italy. Women's wages are half those of men. There are hardly any women in the professions such as medicine, law or ac-

Page 53 Architecture: (*above*) the cathedral at Noto, a fine example of restrained eighteenth-century baroque, built after the 1693 Val di Noto earthquake; (*below*) the cloisters of the Benedictine monastery at Monreale, adjacent to the cathedral. The 216 pairs of columns date from the late twelfth century

Page 54 (*left*) The church of San Sebastiano, Acireale (prov Catania): an example of the ornate late Spanish baroque period; (*below*) Agrigento from the Greek Temple of Juno

countancy. Schoolteaching is the highest achievement of most career-minded girls, but not many are career-minded. Most remain at home until they find a husband, a forlorn hope in the interior villages where most eligible young men have emigrated. Apart from Siracusa and, to a lesser extent, Catania where more emancipated attitudes prevail, courtship is a complicated process that is constrained to take place, at least in the early stages, via intermediaries. Because of limited social contact between the sexes and society's repressive attitude to sex, the male is cast in the role of hunter. Engagements are usually long, although teenage marriages are common and thirty-year-old grandmothers not unknown. Parents have strong influence on the choice of spouse. It is important that the family should not lose prestige in the eyes of the community. Weddings are the opportunity for great ceremony and celebration, even amongst the poor. The smartness and cleanliness of the majority of the rural population are in great contrast to the rather primitive conditions in which many of them live. They like to dress as well as they possibly can in order to generate a measure of respect and to convince themselves that they 'belong' to the village community. Otherwise they could not gather in the piazza or the bar, or take their place in the nightly promenade.

The size of a man's family is still often a matter of jealous pride, an indication of his virility. Moreover the poorer people, who tend to have the largest families, have few other occupations with which to amuse themselves; even in summer it is dark soon after seven. Contraception is, of course, banned by the Church, although some of the urban upper and middle classes practise it. Abortion is also illegal but probably more widespread than the Church would like to admit. Young children, especially boys, are the target of unrestrained emotional affection. Parental discipline is minimal. This adoration of children often approaches idolatry, and is chiefly responsible for the adult male's brash self-assurance and for his violent temper which is essentially that of a spoilt child. Godparenthood is an important custom, functioning often to establish ulterior client relationships under a religious sanction. A mayor or other important local citizen may have hundreds of godchildren. Most people have no more than elementary school education. In most country areas less than 5 per cent of the population have more than five elementary years of schooling, the quality of which, with poor buildings and teaching, is generally low. Although illiteracy has progressively fallen over the decades—it was 89 per cent in 1861 and 40 per cent in 1931—it is still, at 16 per cent of the population over six years of age, twice the Italian average. Many others can read very little and can write little more than their name; these 'semi-illiterates' account for another 22 per cent of the population.

Sicily has three universities, at Palermo, Catania and Messina, each with around 8,000 students, mainly from professional backgrounds. Most of those from country and interior areas are the children of landowners rather than of farmers and peasants. Nearly half the students take degrees in law and jurisprudence; a relative low percentage graduate in rather more useful subjects like economics, engineering or agronomy. Because of lack of jobs, many graduates move to Rome or northern Italy.

The Catholic Church has tremendous power in Sicily, both overall through its connection with politics and administration via the ruling Christian Democrat party, and on a personal scale through the local influence of the priest on village life. Religion in rural areas is a sort of primitive catholicism (for all its ceremony) allied to folklore, magic and the 'evil eye'. Each village and each activity, such as harvesting, fishing or travelling, has its own patron saint. So does each animal and each part of the body. But the Sicilian's view of religion is nothing if not pragmatic, for the revolutionary movements of the *fasci* in the last century and of the socialists and communists today are by no means anticlerical: the image of Christ is carried alongside the red flag.

An example of how religion and the saintly hegemony obtrude

into everyday life is the *festa*. These holidays take place at many times of the year, at Christmas, Easter, at harvest time, and on the commemoration day of the patron saint of each town or village. The *festa* is a phenomenon with its roots deep in history; it demonstrates the very ethos of the Sicilian and the Mediterranean way of life. In the villages like Piana degli Albanesi and the Petralias, where the popular folk culture still survives, traditional costumes are dusted off and resplendently worn by the women. Amidst all the eating, drinking, bawdiness and rejoicing, the religious aspect is never forgotten. Especially at Easter, long processions of people of all ages in traditional and religious costumes wind their way to and from churches. The *festa* is a highly organised affair, run by special committees and financed by a semi-obligatory public subscription. Many festas include fairs, side shows, competitions and horse races.

Puppet shows (*teatro dei pupi*), painted carts and wandering story-tellers belong to a folk tradition that has until recently exhibited an impressive continuity and ability to survive. They may yet be revived, chiefly for touristic interest. The wandering story-teller is occasionally seen in the squares and parks of the big cities, especially around holiday time. Marionette shows, enacting famous scenes from Sicilian history, can still be found around Catania and Acireale. The well-known painted carts have almost everywhere yielded to the scooter-van, but may be seen here and there, especially around the coasts and in the flatter province of Trapani. Some are preserved in the Pitrè Ethnographic Museum in Palermo, and others make scheduled appearances at *festa* time. The painted cart was once the very symbol of rural life. Each village, even each family, had its own special designs. Traditionally the carts were driven on the left of the road, in order to leave the occupant's sword arm free, a custom which caused chaos with motor-traffic using the right-hand side. Folklore and cultural traditions are particularly distinctive in four villages of Albanian origin in the province of Palermo: Piana degli Albanesi (population 7,000), Mezzoiuso

(5,000), Palazzo Adriano (4,000) and Contessa Entellina (3,000).

POVERTY AND UNEMPLOYMENT

Not even the most starry-eyed temple-gazing tourist can deny that there is a great deal of poverty. People are not starving, but perhaps the majority of the peasants and working classes away from the east coast are in varying degrees undernourished, on a diet deficient in protein and minerals. The average per capita income in Sicily is 67 per cent of the Italian average, but behind this figure lies the variation between on the one hand a few very rich people and a growing middle class of moderate wealth, and on the other a large number of very poor people.

According to the official parliamentary reports on poverty and unemployment in Italy published during the 1950s, 25 per cent of the Sicilian population were completely destitute and a further 20 per cent semi-destitute. Severe poverty thus affected almost half the island's population. Of course, it is not in the Sicilian character for the people to bemoan their fate. The sight of laughing bright-eyed children playing in the streets in the hot sun conceals the dreadful conditions in which most of them live.

In Palermo, 200,000 people, a third of the population, are living in serious poverty; 70,000 people live in families without any employment. Unemployment is visible to anyone who has a few hours to wander round the streets during a weekday. Everywhere are groups of men lounging at street corners, in the squares and in the bars. A few yards behind the comfortable homes and fashionable shops of the main streets, a few yards behind the cathedral and the marble courtrooms, one enters a labyrinth of filthy cobbled alleys where the majority of the city's poorer population lives in a honeycomb of rat-infested cellars and windowless rooms.

In western Sicily, 18 per cent of Castellammare's population of 20,000 are officially registered as destitute. This town has an evil reputation, due to its domination by the Mafia and its history of violence under Giuliano's gang of bandits. In 1958 some 80 per cent of Castellammare's adult males had served prison sentences. In southern Sicily many settlements are partly troglodytic. At Licata several hundred, and at Scicli several thousand, peasant families live in caves together with their animals. At Favara, a town burdened with unemployed sulphur miners, 4,000 of the 7,000 families live in one-roomed accommodation, 2,000 of them sharing that one room with animals. The poorest village in Sicily is probably Palma di Montechiaro. Of the 600 families sampled in a 1959 survey, 500 lived in one room only. Infant mortality was 10 per cent, adult illiteracy 70 per cent. The 600 mothers had between them lost 1,014 children, 633 before the age of one year. Over 90 per cent of the houses were without running water, and 86 per cent had no sanitation whatsoever. A quarter of the 3,404 people surveyed slept on the bare floor. Although Palma di Montechiaro is not typical of the whole island, it does indicate the conditions in which some of the poorer Sicilians are constrained to live.

EMIGRATION

Since Unification in 1860, over 2 million Sicilians have left their island; only a third have returned. Emigration has taken place in two distinct phases, the first running up to the First World War; the second starting after the Second World War and continuing to the present day. The causes of the exodus are manyfold, but rest basically on the fact that there has been continual population increase in the face of a stagnant agrarian and virtually non-existent industrial economy. The dominance of America in the early migratory movements is overwhelming. Between 1876 and 1925, 1,279,000—that is, 77 per cent of all Sicilian emigrants—sailed for the USA. A good 90 per cent of the early migrants were peasants or out-of-work agricultural labourers. Comparatively few left the big towns, which were themselves targets for further movement from the depressed, overpopulated countryside. The draining off of unemployed peasants was especially notable at first from communes in the province of Palermo. These communes were nearest to the capital, the chief embarkation point for the New World, but also in a region where the oppressive influences of feudalism and the Mafia were strongest.

There was a tendency for one town or village to send the vast majority of its migrants to just one or possibly two places, so that an expatriate community was formed, with many life-style characteristics of the old community back home. The former inhabitants of Corleone, like many other such emigrant communities, formed associations in New York and New Orleans to expedite the migration and settlement of many of their friends. The inhabitants of Contessa Entellina moved to New Orleans and formed a similar association. The inhabitants of the island of Lipari went to Brooklyn and caused trouble with the authorities by celebrating too vigorously the festival of their patron saint. Much of the early emigration to the USA was clandestine, so that the numbers quoted in official statistics underestimate the flow. Commune census lists often continued to register people long after they had migrated, partly through the laziness of responsible officials, partly because higher populations meant larger official handouts, and partly because many Sicilian emigrants maintain ties with their village, returning home for holidays and periods of work.

Emigration reached its apex in 1913 when 146,061 left Sicily. The emigration epicentre had shifted by this time from the province of Palermo to the province of Trapani. A large proportion of these emigrants, especially those from grape growing areas, went to plant vines in new soil in Tunisia and Algeria. In that single year of 1913, 15 per cent of the inhabitants of Catalafimi left for America or North Africa, 16 per cent of Camporeale, 19 per cent of Salaparuta and Poggioreale, and 22 per cent of Vita.

The second great period of emigration, which started after 1947, has seen an overall diminution in emigration to the USA and a progressive increase within Europe. Whereas before 1925 96 per cent of the emigration was to the Americas, today 70 per cent is to northern Italy and other European countries. The new facts governing Sicilian emigration are those of the remarkable economic boom of north Italian industry, and of the free movement of labour amongst Common Market countries. Ninety-five per cent of the movement to Italy is to the regions of Lombardy, Piedmont, Liguria, Latium and Tuscany, with Milan and Turin the main destinations. Emigrants also go to France, Belgium, Germany, Switzerland and Great Britain, and are often officially assisted. Those going to Germany, for instance, have their fare paid by the Italian government from Sicily to Verona in northern Italy, and by the West German government for the rest of the journey. Work contracts are controlled by EEC regulations to prevent exploitation, and last for six months, one or two years, renewable upon expiry.

Migratory movements continue to be selective and grouped. Little expatriate communities from particular Sicilian villages continue to grow up and flourish in various parts of the world. Emigrants from Ravanusa have clustered at S Etienne-sur-Loire, and those from Randazzo at Lyons and Metz. Numerous former inhabitants of Villalba work in the terraced flower gardens of the Ligurian coast. Fifty men from Realmonte work in the same glassworks in Germany. Numerous families from S Angelo Muxaro work in the brickfields of Bedford. The majority of the emigrants from Enna province have gone to work in the Belgian mines. The inhabitants of Cattolica Eraclea and Ribera have preferred to move to Canada, those of Vizzini and Lingualossa to Australia, those of Balestrate to Venezuela.

In many interior villages half the able-bodied males have emigrated, leaving behind settlements peopled by old folk, women and children; and half these villages' net income comes from emigrant remittances. Generally these remittances are used for the family's subsistence, or saved to enable relatives to join the person who has emigrated. If the money is invested, it is often used to buy land, partly as security for retirement and partly because landownership carries a social prestige value. For the same reasons, when farmers leave Sicily they do not sell their land, nor often their houses, so that uncultivated land and empty, shuttered-up houses remain as a paradox in an island where both agricultural land and accommodation are in terribly short supply. Another aspect of the emigration problem concerns the brain drain. It has been estimated that every year Sicily loses 300 young men of outstandingly high intelligence: men who, if they stayed at home, could become the scientists, educationalists, reformers and entrepreneurs that the island needs.

DANILO DOLCI

No book on contemporary Sicily is complete without mentioning the name of Danilo Dolci, who is perhaps the most important of the group of post-war 'neorealists' bringing to the notice of the world the tragic conditions still existing in Sicily.

Born in 1924 of German-Italian-Slav parentage, Dolci abandoned the prospect of a secure architectural career and moved to Don Zeno's settlement for destitute families near Modena. After two years working there he decided he needed a broader outlook on social problems and visited Trappeto, a small fishing village in western Sicily, which was the poorest place Dolci had ever seen. Soon after his arrival in February 1952, he saw a child die of hunger. He wrote in his diary: 'Before another child starves I wish to die myself.' Dolci suffered a partial paralysis as a result of that first fast, but on the tenth day the authorities promised aid, and Dolci ate. He began to beg and borrow money to feed the needy children. In six months he had acquired a plot of land and built a small home for them. The house was called Borgo di Dio, Village of God. Situated on a hill on the outskirts of Trappeto with enchanting views of the coast, it was the first house in the village to have a bathroom. In 1953 Dolci married Vincenzina, a local widow whose peasant husband had been killed by bandits, leaving her with five children. To these five have been added five more of their own, and a fluctuating number of others whose parents are dead or in prison.

From Trappeto, Dolci moved inland to Partinico where he began the programme of agitation, demonstration, advice, co-operation and inquiry that continues today. His *Centro Studi e Iniziative* occupies a ramshackle collection of rooms that were once part of an old *palazzo* of the landed nobility. In those years of the 1950s the Dolci legend grew famous throughout the world. His fasts in protest against poverty and slum conditions earned him such epithets as the Sicilian Ghandi, 'the colossus of non-violence' (Dolci is an enormous man) and 'the modern St Francis'; whilst on the other hand he was denounced by the authorities as a communist and a troublemaker.

Much of Dolci's energy in the late 1950s and early 1960s was directed to campaigning for a dam on the River Iato. The dam had long been planned but with official hold-ups and no small measure of Mafia opposition it seemed it would never be built. More fasts, demonstrations and protests have at last borne fruit. The dam was constructed between 1963 and 1970, and the tawny valley will soon be green with trees and crops. The reservoir is the largest in Sicily and by 1976 will irrigate 7,000ha. The peasants of several villages, among them Balestrate, Partinico, San Cipirello and San Giuseppe Iato, will benefit enormously if taught to use the water wisely. Dolci and the Partinico centre have been asked by the authorities to build up the consortium of users of the water, about 5,000, and this they are doing, resisting attempts at Mafia infiltration. Dolci is also working on plans for a sports centre round the lake.

Dolci's most famous act was his 'strike in reverse' when he led a group of 150 unemployed to repair a road near Partinico. The police arrested Dolci and carried him away; he was charged with trespass and interference to public property. Dolci remained in jail fifty days before his trial, at which he was sentenced to eight months imprisonment. As soon as work started on the Iato dam in 1963, Dolci began another fast, his eighth, to campaign for a dam on the Belice river to the south.

In recent years Dolci has moved much more from fasting and public demonstrations into the fields of educational and social reform, economic planning and community development. He built up a big organisation of sixty people by 1960; now the team is more streamlined and probably more efficient, with about twenty collaborators. By far the most impressive of Dolci's recent achievements is the new 'Borgo' at Trappeto, a superbly built residential and educational complex near his original Borgo di Dio overlooking the Gulf of Castellammare. A sort of 'Peoples' University'—its official title is the 'Training Centre for Organic Planning'—it provides a medium for the promotion of all sorts of schemes from the regular local meetings of children, fishermen and peasants, to international congresses on community development and rural planning. Special emphasis is placed on residential courses for training elementary school teachers and social workers, and on education through the recreative arts with concerts and exhibitions in which local people participate.

Conceptually the most ambitious recent work of Dolci involves the compilation of a regional development plan for the whole of western Sicily, covering the drainage basins of the Iato, Belice and Carboi rivers. Dolci's dream, fashioned after almost twenty years work and experience in the area, is based on the idea of the 'territory-city'. The aim is to integrate the modernisation of the town and the countryside to meet the real needs of rural Sicilians. This is done by creating nodes of urban and industrial development based on dams, irrigation, orchards, vineyards and vegetable farms. Improved road, port and air transport facilities would connect the area with local and mainland markets. Agrarian reforms, co-operative and credit schemes would provide for assembling and dispersing capital and resources. The immediate objectives of the plan are to double the present income level and create a productive cycle of work and activity for men and women of all ages. Dolci is enthusiastic about the plan: 'In London you can live but hardly breathe; in India you can breathe but hardly live; here you can both live and breathe. Here there is the possibility of creating a new kind of life.'

Danilo Dolci still remains the founder and procurator of all new hope in western Sicily. But certain aspects of his organisational ability, his autocracy, his unwillingness to suffer fools gladly and devote time to people who cannot be of real service to him and his cause have resulted in some of his disciples eventually turning against him. Part of the reason for the internal controversies has been Dolci's refusal to ally his work with any political party. Although Dolci may be politically naive, his aims are not political; they are social, educative and economic. He continues to be harassed by the most powerful groups in Sicily, the Christian Democrat Party, the Mafia, and the Catholic Church. In spite of all this, Dolci's independent soul goes marching on and, although bereft of official recognition and financial support from the Italian and Sicilian authorities, there are signs that this is changing. Dolci's work is supported by Italian committees in Rome, Milan and Turin, by groups in Germany, Holland, France, Norway, Denmark and Finland, and by three national committees, a Swiss one, a British one, and, most active of all, a Swedish committee which provided much of the money for the new Borgo at Trappeto.

5   INDUSTRY AND TRADE

IT seems that Unification with Italy dealt a severe blow to any process of incipient industrialisation that Sicily might have been experiencing. In the early nineteenth century Sicily had a textile industry, at Palermo, Trapani, and Messina, that was, if anything, more advanced than that of the mainland. Cotton was grown locally and the production of fine woollens was possible after the introduction of merino sheep in 1820. Two factories at Messina were said to employ a thousand people each, all female labour, using flying shuttles, and Arkwright cotton mills were in operation by the 1830s. There was a thriving silk industry in the north-east based at Messina. Palermo had the Orotea iron foundry (using imported ore) employing 800 workers, with allied shipbuilding industries. Other industrial development at this time was linked to agricultural produce: wine-making at Trapani, Marsala and Vittoria, the conservation of tuna fish on Favignana, oil-milling, the production of pasta and cheeses, etc. Official figures give 35 per cent of the working population as employed in industry in 1861, but the vast majority of these people were artisans working alone or in small workshops. Today artisan activity is collapsing, its economy destroyed by the penetration of cheap north Italian manufactured goods to all parts of the island. It can only be reprieved by the growth of a tourist market. This is happening in Taormina, for example, where every other shop sells handicraft goods, dolls and souvenirs. Over half of the island's 460,000 industrial workers currently work in mining and the building industry. The classical industries like salt and sulphur have been producing uninterrupted for thousands of years, but are purely extractive and have benefited the economy in only a limited sense.

SULPHUR MINING

The mining of sulphur took place in Greek and Roman times, and continued throughout the Middle Ages and the medieval period. It reached its apex during the last century, when Sicily produced over three-quarters of the world's supply. The majority of the mines were, and still are, located in a broad belt some 100km long by about 40km broad running along the axis from Agrigento to Enna and Caltanissetta. Annual production of raw sulphur rose from 200,000 tons in 1870 to 500,000 tons by 1900, when over 50,000 people worked in the mines. Output has fairly steadily fallen since the early 1900s and now competes with difficulty on world markets; on occasions in recent

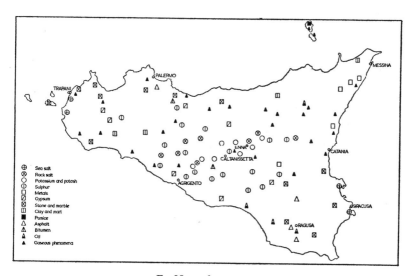

E   Natural resources

years as much as 230,000 tons—over two years' supply—has been stockpiled at the mines and on the quaysides at Porto Empedocle and Termini Imerese.

From 105 mines in 1957 (there were 800 in 1904) the number has fallen to less than fifty. Of these only nineteen are listed for mechanisation and modernisation; the rest—which, incidentally, have the poorest safety standards of any mines in Europe—will gradually close down, and in fact half the output now comes from just four mines: Trabia, Trabonella, Cozzo Disi and Montagna Mintini. The number of miners is likewise being reduced, from 10,000 in 1955 to fewer than 6,000 in 1965. Ultimately, according to present plans, there will be only 2,800. Sicily now produces no more than 2 per cent of the world's sulphur.

OIL

Small-scale indications of the existence of hydrocarbons—in solid, liquid and gas forms—have been known for many centuries. Small pools of petroleum (used for lamps) and frequent eruptions of gas from mud vents and fissures had long been noted in the clay zones, and the asphalt deposits have been exploited throughout the island's history. Exploration for commercial oil deposits is more recent, limited to the present century. Early drillings progressed slowly; the real impulse came after the Second World War, and in 1953 the American Gulf Oil Company struck oil in commercial quantities near Ragusa. Production began here in 1954. In 1956 the state hydrocarbons organisation, ENI, discovered a field near Gela, extending out under the sea, and BP found a further source near Ragusa. Sicily soon became responsible for the major part of the Italian oil industry and hopes rose high for further and better discoveries in the island. By 1958 two-thirds of Sicily were under concession to oil companies for exploration rights. Production grew initially: 1·1 million tons in 1957, 1·7 in 1963; but then fell back to 1·1 by 1970, although Sicily still produces 90 per cent of Italy's total domestic oil output.

If Sicilian oil never fulfilled its early promise, some considerable developments have nevertheless resulted. Great refining complexes have arisen on the south and east coasts, and Sicily's central location in the Mediterranean has made it easy to import crude oil from the Middle East, especially North Africa, and Russia. Nowadays, with the closure of the Suez Canal, the majority of the supply (25 million tons in 1969) comes from near-by Libya. In 1957 the Ragusa oilfield was linked by pipeline to a refinery at Augusta, which today has a capacity of 8 million tons of crude per year. Even greater things transpired at Gela, although the local oil is deeper, heavier and more expensive to extract. Gela's petro-chemicals complex, in operation by 1964, not only includes refineries and allied processing industries, but also a completely new port and a 5km jetty to a deepsea terminal where large foreign tankers can discharge. This artificial floating island—called Scarabeo—is unique in Europe. Lit up at night to enable round-the-clock docking, this shining beacon of the world's new technical age seems centuries remote from the life the majority of Sicilians still lead. The Gela complex now covers four sectors of petroleum activity: a refinery concentrating on heavy oil products like benzine; a petro-chemicals industry; a fertilisers plant and a thermo-electric power plant. Other refineries—at Ragusa, Milazzo and Termini Imerese—bring crude refining capacity up to a total of well over 20 million tons per year.

An even more recent development is the use of methane gas for industry and domestic purposes. Gas pipelines have been laid to connect the important Gagliano (province of Enna) gas field north to Termini Imerese and Palermo and south to Porto Empedocle. A second gas find at Bronte, just west of Etna, is piped through to Catania, and methane at Marzara del Vallo and Lippone in the west is fed directly into the domestic supply.

OTHER MINERALS

Sicily has at various times been mined for several other minerals. The Peloritani Mountains, the island's oldest and most metalliferous rocks, have been combed for silver, copper, antimony and associated metals. Rocks currently quarried commercially include chalk, clays and marls in the southern interior, and most importantly marble and building stone, especially at Comiso and Ragusa (limestone) and around Trapani (marble and other decorative rocks).

Rock salt is mined in several different localities in the centre of the island, especially north-east of Enna and north of Agrigento, but production is low compared to marine salt. Salt pans are concentrated around the Trapani-Marsala area, where 87 per cent of the island's salt is produced, and on the east coast at Augusta. Methods may be centuries old, but they are indeed picturesque. Everything is blue and white: blue sea, blue sky, white houses, and conical mounds of sun-white salt. Old wind-pumps, starkly vertical in a flat landscape, lift water from one pan to another. Little flat-bottomed boats transport the product along narrow, white-banked canals towards Trapani. Modernisation comes slowly. The 1,200 men who work in the salt basins during the four months of summer, when the sun is at its evaporating best, still carry 30kg baskets of salt on their shoulders from the pans to the heaps at the canal-side. But such methods cannot survive indefinitely in a world of fierce competition. Production is falling, from 190,000 tons in 1938 to 187,000 in 1950 and to less than 150,000 tons in recent years.

Other important minerals are asphalt and potash. Asphalt and bitumen are semi-solid forms of oil and are used for distillation of oils and road surfacing. The chief quarries are around Ragusa, at Scicli, between Vizzini and Licodia Eubea, and farther north near Caltagirone. A distillation plant for the production of heavy lubricating oil was built at Ragusa before

Page 71   (above) The Greek theatre at Segesta in western Sicily. The clay and limestone landscape is typical of that of the interior; (below) Erice: the ruined Norman castle at the eastern end of the hilltop town

Page 72 Agriculture and irrigation: (*above*) the summer flow of the largest river in Sicily, the Simeto. The span of the bridge gives an idea of its winter maximum; (*below*) newly planted citrus groves in the middle Simeto valley near Paternò

the Second World War, but nowadays most of the limited production goes to the newer, larger petro-chemicals plants or to making road metal. Potash is found in strata immediately above those bearing sulphur. Potassic compounds (kainite) were discovered in 1951 and production commenced in 1957. The Montecatini Company found a large bed at Serradifalco, and then others at Racalmuto and Nicosia. Other companies exploring the Sicilian sulphur region (Misab, Edison—now merged with Montecatini into Montedison—and the Trinacria Society) found significant deposits at Calascibetta, Santa Catarina Villarmosa, Montedoro, Corvillo, Pasquasia and a few other places. Production of kainite rose from 60,000 tons in 1958 to surpass 1 million tons in 1962 and is now approaching 3 million tons. Some initial refining is carried out at the mines, but a number of plants for further refining into potassium sulphate have recently been built at strategic points on transport axes and where water is available for the refining process. The Montecatini Company has set up the largest potash complex— the so-called 'triangle of potassium', with vertices at San Cataldo, Campofranco and Porto Empedocle. From the San Cataldo mines 3km north of Serradifalco the kainite is transported 18km in hoppers along an aerial wireway across the deserted grainlands to the chemicals plant at Campofranco in the Platani valley. Here it is processed into potassium sulphate and taken by road or rail the 33km to Porto Empedocle, where the new Akragas plant transforms the mineral into various types of fertiliser for export.

THE DEVELOPMENT OF MANUFACTURING INDUSTRY

A critical factor in the development of secondary industry has been the availability of power. Before 1947 electricity was in private hands, its supply limited and its price high. With the placing of the service under the public control of the *Ente Siciliano di Elettricità* production from both thermal (oil and coal-fired) and hydro sources has expanded dramatically. In 1955 Sicily was connected to the mainland electricity grid by means of a $3\frac{1}{2}$km power line across the Straits of Messina. The six overhead cables (soon to be doubled) connecting the giant pylons enable the mainland to supplement the island's still inadequate supplies. Sicily now possesses 49 thermal stations with a combined capacity of 1,128,400kW and 40 hydroelectric power stations with a total of 234,600kW. Typical of the dual-purpose hydro schemes is the reservoir of Piana degli Albanesi on the River Hône, built as long ago as 1923: with a head of 500 metres this provides an energy output of 18 million kWh, as well as supplying valuable irrigation water to the Conca d'Oro.

Recent industrialisation in Sicily, particularly manufacturing, must also be viewed within the context of regional government and national policy. After 1950, various tax exemptions and financial incentives were offered to industry locating in Southern Italy, and after about 1957 the *Cassa per il Mezzogiorno*, the government special agency for developing the south, turned its attention from providing purely agricultural and infrastructural developments to helping industrial growth too. Sicily and Sardinia, having a measure of autonomy, were rather special cases, and their regional governments were able to plan for and encourage industrialisation over and above the national southern policy. Three special agencies were set up for administering credit and financial help to Sicilian industry: IRFIS (*Istituto Regionale per il Finanziamento alle Industrie Siciliane*) in 1952, SOFIS (*Società Finanziaria dell'Industria in Sicilia*) in 1958, and most recently ESPI (*Ente Siciliano per la Promozione Industriale*). Furthermore, following the development of 'growth pole' theory in economics, several localities were selected as industrial development nuclei: these include all the provincial capitals except Enna and a few other towns as well (ie Trapani, Palermo, Agrigento-Porto Empedocle, Caltanissetta, Ragusa, Messina, Catania, Siracusa-Augusta, Gela, Caltagirone). In only a few cases, however, have the municipalities concerned succeeded in providing the necessary infrastructures and land purchases for the setting up of industrial estates. Apart from Gela and Ragusa, only two industrial zones have readily developed: at Catania where an industrial estate has grown up in recent years on the flat land to the south of the city, and at Siracusa-Augusta, where developments are on a scale that is European or Mediterranean rather than purely local. Elsewhere, at Palermo, Messina, Trapani and the other nuclei, with the partial exception of Porto Empedocle, industrialisation is not taking place, or only slowly, and the towns are stagnating.

The geographical factors for the location of industry along the eastern seaboard, especially between Augusta and Siracusa, are extremely favourable: they include proximity of raw materials including oil, sulphur, potassium and salts; plenty of flat land for factory building along the coast; excellent deep water harbours able to accommodate the world's largest cargo ships and tankers; the coastal railway line leading north to Messina; a motorway that has recently been completed along the same route; useful location for the import of Middle East oil and North African iron ore, and for the exploitation of the growing markets of the semi-developed countries bordering the Mediterranean; and finally the important human advantages of a fairly resourceful and Mafia-free local population. The industries of the Augusta-Siracusa axis employ 15,000 persons, over a third of whom work in chemicals. Half the workers live in Siracusa, but a commuter movement from the surrounding villages to the coastal industries is a growing phenomenon.

Expansion of the oil-based industries as the backbone of future industrial development has been recommended. Petroleum by-products earmarked for development include plastics and synthetic resins, rubbers, detergents, insecticides and paints. Expansion of the cement industry is a necessary adjunct to the factory and housebuilding programme, and production will rise to $1\frac{1}{2}$ million tons by 1975. A wider range of food-processing industries is also to be introduced, but the most ambitious new departures are likely to be the establishment of a non-ferrous metals refining industry based on imported ores of aluminium, lead, zinc and copper, and the consequent progression to mechanical engineering industries. All of this means that Augusta, whose port activity was virtually zero in 1952, is about to become Italy's second largest port, after Genoa, in terms of tonnage handled. Freight trade in Sicily's traditionally largest ports—Palermo, Messina and Trapani—is stagnating, having been overtaken in recent years by Gela and Porto Empedocle, again ports that were virtually non-existent twenty years ago.

Other recent industrial developments are more modest. Catania's industrial estate, located on 3sq km of flat land adjacent to the airport and between the railway and the main road to Siracusa, is more a natural outgrowth of a city with a long-established commercial and industrial tradition. In contrast to Siracusa-Augusta, here the emphasis is on small and medium manufacturing firms—over fifty of them to date—producing a wide variety of goods mostly for the Sicilian market, and working independently of each other. At present 4,000 operatives are employed; when the expansion of the estate is complete work will be provided for 10,000.

At Milazzo, there are plans for a lubricants plant alongside the *Società Mediterranea* oil refinery, and for enlarging the port to deal with larger tankers. Pirelli-Dunlop is expanding its rubber plant at Villafranca Tirrena, between Messina and Milazzo, concentrating on production of heavy vehicle tyres; also near Messina the Patti cement plant is to be enlarged. A pilot scheme for the production of knitwear and hosiery has been set up at Licata by a subsidiary of the Montedison group. Perhaps the most important recent manufacturing development has been the opening in 1970 of Fiat's car assembly plant employing 800 workers at Termini Imerese, east of Palermo, which incorporates an investment of £200 million ($480 million). Another Sicilian industry worth noting is the Rodriquez shipyard at Messina, the world's largest and most successful builder of hydrofoils. The yard employs 400 workers and has built over a hundred hydrofoils since 1956. The largest, costing around £400,000 ($1 million), carry 140 passengers at 50 knots. As well as plying from Messina to the mainland and out to the Eolian Isles, Rodriquez hydrofoils are in service all over the world. One has even played an important part in a James Bond film!

In general, however, industrial development does not give cause for great satisfaction or optimism. The efforts of the regional government and the *Cassa per il Mezzogiorno* have not brought results commensurate with the massive financial input. The Sicilian industrial association, *Sicilindustrie*, claims that employment in the industrial sector is declining and points out that Sicily alone in Italy has a lower percentage of people engaged in industry now than in 1951. The 1961 Industrial Census showed that two-thirds of industrial employees were in concerns of fewer than ten persons each. Most of Sicily's burgeoning industries are highly capital-intensive, and most of the profits produced go to Northern Italy whence came the original investment. The many studies of the industrialising communities of south-east Sicily emphasise that development is qualitative rather than quantitative. The type of industrialisation taking place can employ only a proportion of the population thrown up by natural increase alone—emigration must therefore continue—and moreover the cultural problems provoked by living and working in a suddenly up-to-date technological environment impose severe strains on a society which still has many antique traditions and in which educational attainment is often very low. The most significant geographical problem is that development has been highly localised to the south-eastern corner of the island. Industry and trade in Palermo are if anything in decline. Foreign and North Italian capital is reluctant to move into a city where attitudes of mind are difficult to change and where Mafia influence is strong.

Palermo's biggest industry, the *Cantieri Navali del Tirreno e Riuniti* shipyards, has recently been taken over by the Italian state holding group IRI (*Istituto per la Ricostruzione Industriale*) after a financial crisis in 1969 and a two-month strike by the 2,300 labour force in 1970.

To what extent Sicily will be able to plan for economic and industrial development in the future is largely a matter of conjecture. Economic planning, or at least the activation of such planning, has yet to get off the ground. A special ministerial office for economic planning has been established in Palermo, but this is only a stop-gap measure. The problem remains whether the Rome government will ever accept as legitimate, and financially support, a Sicilian economic development plan and, if it does, whether the Sicilian government's administrative resources are sufficiently free of corruption and conflicting interests to be able to carry it through.

6 TRANSPORT AND COMMUNICATIONS

ROADS

THE roads are of three categories: State roads, having a number prefaced by 'SS' for *Strada Statale*, the responsibility of the Italian government; provincial roads, maintained by the provincial administrations; and commune roads, the responsibility of local villages. Twenty-four per cent are State roads, 63 per cent provincial and only 10 per cent commune roads; the indication is that most communes are too poor to be able to build and surface their own roads. For centuries, the only routeways for most parts of central Sicily were *mulattiere* or rocky mule tracks, and *trazzere*, the much wider communal routes used for transhumant sheep movements. After Unification the national government started an energetic roadbuilding programme, and between 1860 and the First World War several important routes were built: the Palermo–Messina road along the north coast; the south coast road, and the principal trans-island links—between Palermo and Sciacca, Palermo and Agrigento, between Santo Stefano di Camastra and Gela via Nicosia and Enna, and between Enna and Agrigento via Caltanissetta and Canicattì. By 1910 the Sicilian road network contained 7,781km. During the next forty years development was very slow, the network increasing by only 11 per cent to 8,619km, but the increase in road length was 33 per cent over the period 1950–64. Today there are more than 13,000km, a density of nearly 500km per 1,000sq km.

Most traffic passes along the main east coast trunk route between Messina and Siracusa, where the average daily flow is over 10,000 passengers, reaching 20,000 around Catania and north of Siracusa. The only other comparably busy stretch of road is round the Conca d'Oro between Palermo and Ficarazzi. The other principal traffic axes, carrying 5,000–10,000 passengers per day, are between Catania and Enna, Enna and Gela, and those focusing on Agrigento and Porto Empedocle. The main north coast road carries surprisingly little traffic. Some State roads in the interior, especially those crossing the Nebrodi Mountains, carry fewer than 500 people daily.

Nevertheless the road sector is one that is increasing rapidly. New by-passes are built, round Modica, Lentini and Agrigento for instance; tortuous bends are straightened by embankments and cuttings, and remaining gravel stretches on the more main roads are being metalled. A recently built road bridge passing 150m above a ravine at Modica claims to be the highest concrete bridge in Europe. A 25km stretch of motorway from Palermo to its airport at Punta Raisi has been open for several years, and two other major motorways, between Messina and Catania, and Palermo and Catania, have recently been opened. If the Straits of Messina link is ever constructed it will be possible to drive from Catania or Palermo straight on to the *Autostrada del Sole*, which runs the length of Italy and connects up with the European motorway network.

RAILWAYS

Sicily's railways are virtually part of the mainland network, for the wagons run on to lengths of track on the deck of the train ferry across the Straits of Messina, and are hauled off at the other side. The 'Peloritani Express' runs from Rome to Palermo in 11¼ hours. At Messina the train divides, one half going along the north coast to Palermo, and the other half going south to Catania and Siracusa. There are through carriages to these places from Turin, Milan and Venice, and from Rome to Trapani, Agrigento (via Catania and Caltanissetta), and Vittoria (via Siracusa, Modica and Ragusa). There are three principal axes of passenger movement within Sicily (with more than twenty passenger trains per day): Messina–Palermo, Messina–Siracusa and Catania–Agrigento. The busiest stretch of all is Palermo–Fiumetorto with over thirty. The branch lines, especially Noto–Pachino and Motta Sant'Angelo–Regalbuto, have very few services, only a couple of trains per day.

The siting of many Sicilian settlements on hill-tops and steep mountain-sides makes access by railway difficult if not impossible. This applies not only to the villages but also to a provincial capital like Enna, whose station is in the valley 300m below the town. Alighting at a railway station in deserted countryside, the confused foreign traveller is relayed to an often unseen hillside town by bus. The stations of Montemaggiore Belsito and Butera, for instance, are 15km from their respective settlements. Marianopoli station is 8km to the north of the village, whilst the railway itself passes 100m directly underneath the village in a 6km tunnel!

The first railway in Sicily was opened in 1863, a short stretch of 13km between Palermo and Bagheria. Two routes were planned initially, one running from Palermo south to Lercara Bassa and on to Porto Empedocle, the other running north-south along the east coast from Messina to Siracusa. The Messina line, although started later, was built faster as it was a natural prolongation of the Calabrian line also being built; the 95km between Messina and Catania was built during 1866 and extended to Siracusa in 1869. This line down the west coast of Calabria and the east coast of Sicily is one of the most scenic in Europe, running through a succession of citrus and olive groves and irrigated gardens, with views on the one hand to the sea and on the other to high rugged mountains.

New railway building laws in 1870 led to more lines, chief

among these being a cross-island link between the two original north-south routes. In 1885 the Sicilian Railway Company took over control of some of the island's railways. Four new lines were projected: along the north coast between Messina and Palermo (joining the Palermo–Porto Empedocle route at Fiumetorto); from Siracusa across the south-eastern corner of the island to Gela and thence to Licata; from Valsavoia (between Catania and Siracusa) inland to Caltagirone; and westwards from Porto Empedocle to Castelvetrano (not started for another twenty-five years because of routing disputes). The most important of these new railways was the Messina–Fiumetorto line, completed in 1895, in time for the first express passenger locomotives to run (top speed 85kph). The Valsavoia branch was opened to Scordia in 1889 and to Caltagirone in 1892. More interesting is the Siracusa–Licata line, especially the Siracusa–Gela section which crosses a stepped plateau-ravine topography, one of the most awkward for railway construction. This line meanders in a most haphazard fashion, taking great curves into deserted countryside, particularly between Ragusa and Comiso. For 9km between Scicli and Modica the line runs in a ravine, but this is nothing compared with the contortions necessary to reach Ragusa at 500m; in one place the line loops the loop, running in a circle back under itself.

In 1881 the *Ferrovie Sicule Occidentali*, in response to requests from the Palermo and Trapani provincial governments, opened a 194km standard gauge route between Palermo and Trapani. Another line, this time narrow gauge, south from Palermo to Corleone (68km) was opened by 1886, and extended, in 1903, a further 40km to San Carlo. The line proved impossibly uneconomic and closed in 1959.

The most fascinating railway line in Sicily must be the *Circumetnea*, opened in 1895 and still, thanks to an increasing flow of tourist passengers, hard at work. Starting at Riposto on the eastern, coastal side of Etna, the line describes a 113km loop round the great volcano, ending up at Catania. Lingualossa, Randazzo, Bronte, Adrano, Biancavilla, Paternò and Misterbianco are some of the villages and country towns served by the line, which meanders through gardens, vineyards, orchards, and across the occasional sterile lava field. On the section between Bronte and Adrano there is nothing but forest and lava between the railway and the volcano's summit. In 1923 a lava flow cut the line just west of Lingualossa, burying it beneath 10m of molten rock. After working in two halves for four years a new loop was constructed round the tongue of the solidified lava taking the route via Castiglione and adding 7km to the length of the track. In 1952 the old route was resumed by cutting through the 1923 lava, leaving the loop obsolete, except for the western branch to Castiglione which was used for freight until 1961. Another lava outpouring occurred in 1928, threatening the line above Giarre. Lava filled a ravine bridged by the line, but then conveniently cooled, so that new track could be laid across solid rock and there was one less bridge to maintain. Farther down, the lava caused more serious trouble to the Messina–Catania main line, smothering a section at Mascali, including the station, to a depth of 15m. Since 1928 the *Circumetnea* has had no more trouble from lava flows, and was unaffected by the 1971 eruption.

In 1905 Sicilian railways were nationalised under the *Ferrovie dello Stato* (FS), the Italian State Railways. Diesel railcars, ideally suited to the steep gradients, appeared in 1935. A short branch line was opened between Noto and Pachino in 1934, and another from Motta Sant'Angelo to Schettino soon after (extended to Regalbuto in 1949). A shorter north-west coast link, from Alcamo Diramazione to Trapani (passing the Segesta temple) opened in 1938. In 1959 a railway from Alcantara to Randazzo was completed, like the Motta Sant'Angelo–Regalbuto line running parallel to the *Circumetnea* but lower down the slope, and a new route from Caltagirone to Gela is at present under construction.

Although the FS would like to close down some of the more recently built branch lines, no standard gauge route has yet been closed. The lines that are in serious difficulty are the 462km of narrow gauge network. The growth of road services, in particular bus travel and scooter and car ownership, is finally killing these lines off one by one. The two main sections of narrow gauge still operating are the *Circumetnea* and the line from Porto Empedocle to Castelvetrano and Santa Ninfa—a combined total of 226km. Santa Ninfa–Salemi closed in 1954, Agrigento–Licata and Canicattì in 1958, followed by the much longer Palermo–San Carlo and Lercara Bassa–Magazzolo in 1959.

The opening and closing of various lines over the past fifty years has caused the total network—standard and narrow gauges—to fluctuate considerably in length. From 1,563km in 1912, total track length grew to 2,182km in 1938, but fell to 1,681km by 1961. Soon, with double tracking of the island's busiest stretches and the completion of the Caltagirone–Gela line, the network will increase to over 1,800km. Palermo–Fiumetorto and Catania–Bicocca are the only double-track sections to date. Since 1950 the FS has been working on electrification of the main lines. The main Palermo–Messina line was electrified in 1951–5 and the Messina–Siracusa in 1958–60.

COMMUNICATIONS ACROSS THE STRAITS OF MESSINA

Boats have plied across the 3km Messina Straits—the legendary Straits of Scylla and Charybdis—with some regularity at least since classical times. With the Unification of Italy the setting up of time-tabled services and the possible establishment of a more permanent link assumed political urgency. Two paddle steamers, called appropriately *Scilla* and *Cariddi*, each transporting three railway passenger coaches, were brought into service between Messina and Reggio Calabria (a 15km crossing) in 1899. In 1905 a new train-ferry dock was opened at Villa

San Giovanni north of Reggio, reducing the sea crossing to 7km, and two larger ships, the *Sicilia* and the *Calabria*, were brought into service.

Wagon-units (large passenger coaches and locomotives equal two wagon-units) crossing the Straits increased from 39,000 in 1906 to 155,000 in 1929, and up to nearly 700,000 per annum at the present time. Sixty passenger coaches are now ferried across each day, and a large part of the Sicilian orange and lemon crop, as well as other exports, are conveyed by freight wagons destined for North Italian and European stations. The FS now has ten train ferries in operation, with capacities varying between 20 and 43 wagon-units each. Two vessels, the *Villa* and the *Messina*, have been converted to carry road vehicles, the most rapidly increasing ferry traffic of recent years. The two largest train ferries, the *Ignazia* and the *Sibari*, each of 43 wagon capacity, were put into service in 1969. Messina now has seven train-ferry docks, Villa four and Reggio two. The crossing to Villa takes 35 minutes, that to Reggio 55 minutes. About 9 million passengers are currently ferried across the Straits each year, compared with 5 million in 1958 and 3¾ million in 1950. Eighty-six per cent of both the passenger and freight traffic across the Straits is destined for Villa and the Tyrrhenian coast road and rail routes that lead most directly to Naples, Rome and the north; only 14 per cent passes via Reggio Calabria along the Ionian coast routes to Taranto, Bari, etc. To cope with the ever increasing flow of traffic there is now also a private car and passenger service, and several smaller, faster craft serving traffic demands of a local nature.

The idea of a more permanent link between Sicily and the mainland—a bridge or tunnel—has been much discussed since the Second World War. Like the crossing of the English Channel, the dream is more than a hundred years old, and over a hundred schemes have been put forward. A recent adaptation on the tunnel alternative, following subaqua geological and current surveys by Jacques Cousteau, calls for an immersed tube tunnel. A semi-flexible tube resting on the seabed would be cheaper than a conventional subterranean tunnel and, more importantly, it would be less liable to earthquake damage.

The most recent proposal is for an imposing dual-purpose bridge connecting Santa Agata and Punta Pezzo, the shortest crossing of just under 3km. It will be a suspension bridge on two levels, the upper for road and the lower for rail. The advantages for freight and passenger movements will obviously be enormous. Half a million vehicles make the crossing each year and in some years large quantities of fruit have gone rotten on the quayside at Messina awaiting the ferry. But the cost will be enormous (about £500 million; $1,200 million), and there are strong arguments for an improved ferry service, with perhaps a third crossing route, instead. As long ago as 1955 an Italian government publication announced that 'work on the building of the greatest bridge in the world is about to begin'. Construction has still not started and it will probably be many years, even decades, before the dream becomes a reality, before the bridge that separates two worlds is built.

7 MAJOR CITIES AND TOWNS

A FASCINATING mixture of modern commerce and oriental bazaar, of architectural wonder and rubbish-dump, of cultural splendour and primitive squalor, Palermo is the capital of Sicily and the sixth largest city in Italy. One of the great ports of the Mediterranean, with a population of 625,000, it is well situated on the island's north coast, surrounded by a fertile plain and protected from the north winds by Monte Pellegrino.

A necropolis at the foot of this mountain pushes the date of original settlement back into the Neolithic, but it seems the city was founded in the sixth century BC by the Phoenicians. It became the chief centre of the Carthaginians in Sicily until 254 BC when it fell to the Romans. In AD 831 Palermo was taken by the Saracens after much destruction and killing. Recovery was rapid, however, and under the Arabs the city was made the island's capital and attained great prosperity. The Arabs built new quarters, in the form of the tightly packed labyrinths of streets and courtyards characteristic of moslem culture. The most important extension was the Kalsa, meaning 'the elect', built east of the old town in the tenth century, to accommodate the Arabs' military forces.

After the Normans the city declined, but great rebuilding and replanning took place under the Spanish viceroys. The Via Vittorio Emanuele and the Via Maqueda, still the two great thoroughfares of the city, were driven straight as a dye through the tangled knot of Arab-style Palermo. They crossed at the

Quattro Canti, a focal point of the city today. Although much of the oriental remains, the overwhelming impression of the main streets is given by the *palazzi* of the Spanish period after about 1600. Such learned institutions as the astronomical observatory, the botanical garden (famous for its tropical flora) and the university were founded during the later Spanish period, and by the end of the seventeenth century the city contained thirty-eight convents, thirty-nine monasteries and 152 churches, for a grand total 7,379 nuns, monks and priests! Palermo, with 400,000 inhabitants, was then the second city of Italy after Naples.

The nineteenth century saw a further expansion, in the form of new suburbs and villas. Rapid population growth in the old city caused increasing overcrowding. The city's area trebled during the period 1860–1910. Recent growth is due partly to a continuing high birth-rate and partly to the influx of migrants (over 4,000 per year) from other parts of the island, only a relatively small proportion of whom, however, find satisfaction and permanent employment. Perhaps no other city in Europe has such a proliferation of petty traders, loafers and pickpockets. In the 1961 Industrial Census, 44,500 men did not belong to any recognised category of work. For the most part they are concentrated in or near the city centre, in the slums that lie concealed just behind the broad main streets, in the Kalsa and at the foot of M Pellegrino. Remarkably little is known about the sociology of Sicilian back street life. The Kalsa has increasingly become the refuge of the very poor awaiting work and rehousing. This, and other quarters like Albergheria, Cortile Cascino, Pozzo della Morte and Ballarò are slowly being cleared. Part of the Albergheria remains as the home of the horse-drawn taxi drivers; the smell of the *carozza* stables is unmistakable. There are over 600 horse carts in the city; they remain partly as a tourist attraction and partly as something unique to the city, even though they hold up traffic and are insanitary. Very different is the newer city, developed north

Page 89 Industry: (*above*) the fishing quarter of Palermo; fishing remains an important activity and Sicilian fishermen follow a distinctive way of life; (*below*) landscapes of sulphur: panorama of a sulphur mine still at work near Caltanissetta

Page 90   Derelict sulphur mine in the province of Caltanissetta; pithead gear, buildings and trucks, all lying disused, bear witness to the decline of the industry

from the line of the Via Cavour, Via Volturno and Corso Finocchiaro Aprile towards the fashionable bathing resort of Mondello. Here are wide, tree-planted streets, lively piazzas and considerable areas of parkland like the Giardino Inglese. Palermo's industrial estate is still in the planning stage, only 45ha having been obtained at Brancaccio on the south side of the city: too small for modern industrial development of any significance and too costly in the midst of rich gardens and orchards. The only sectors of the city's economy that are developing are public administration and service industry, which between them employ 27 per cent of the working population. In spite of the poverty, the cramped living conditions of maybe half its population, and the stranglehold the Mafia still has on aspects of its life and economy, Palermo is one of the world's most beautiful cities.

MESSINA

Messina is the least Sicilian, or the most 'Italian', of all the island's towns. Its location obviously makes it more open to external contacts. The short stretch of intervening water is less of a barrier than the rocky Peloritani Mountains that reach 1,000m within 6km of the coast and virtually isolate Messina from the rest of Sicily. Six kilometres long and only one broad, it is a city of the sea, and little else. Fifty ferry-boats and twenty hydrofoils cross the Straits each day, giving a daily movement of local population of 20,000. In contrast to the last century, industry in Messina is poorly developed. The assembly of refrigerators, the hydrofoil yard, brewing and the making of fruit juices do not constitute a great deal of employment. To the north and south of Messina, small fishing, agricultural and resort villages have grown up—some with names like 'peace' (Pace) and 'paradise' (Paradiso)—so that the city fades much less abruptly into the surrounding countryside than most Sicilian towns.

F

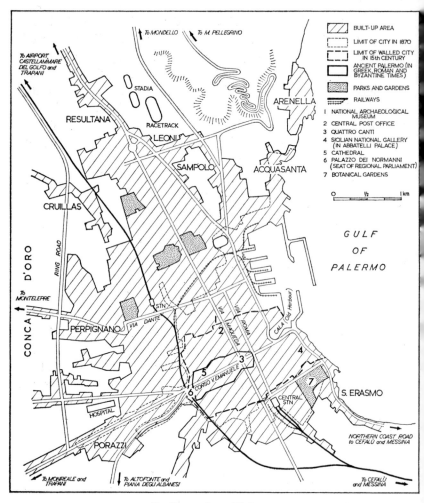

F   Street plan of Palermo

Messina was founded in the eighth century BC by settlers
from Cumae on the mainland and from nearby Naxos. Greek,
Roman, Byzantine, Arab, Norman, Spanish and modern
Messina all experienced fluctuating developments. Perhaps the
major period of prosperity started with the Crusaders—
Richard I of England and Philip Augustus of France wintered
here in 1190–1 en route for Palestine—and continued through
till the fourteenth century. During this period the city was one
of the major trading centres of the Mediterranean, with communities of Genoese, Pisans, Venetians and Jews. By 1650 the
population had reached 70,000, but was decimated by plagues
of cholera in 1743 and again in 1854. In 1783 an earthquake
killed 30,000 in Messina and the surrounding villages. By 1800
the population was below 50,000. The city suffered greatly
from Spanish misrule and was heavily bombarded by Ferdinand
II in 1848. On 28 December 1908, in one of the world's largest
and most cruel earthquakes, Messina was entirely destroyed
and 80,000 people were killed. Reconstruction work was far
from complete when, in the Second World War, 30,000 bombs
reduced the city to rubble once more, killing 5,000 citizens.

One or two buildings of note did survive: the twelfth-
century church of Annunziata dei Catalani, the Vittorio
Emanuele Theatre (1852) and the Orion Fountain in the Piazza
Duomo. The cathedral is a twentieth-century reconstruction of
the original Norman building; a doorway remains and there are
thirteenth-century mosaics in the interior. The campanile contains the largest astronomical clock in the world. Present-day
Messina has a population of 200,000 and extends over an area
three times as great as the pre-earthquake city; part of the
reason for the spread being the need to build low, antiseismic
buildings.

CATANIA

Situated where the slopes of Etna meet the sea, Catania has the
appearance of a prosperous north Italian city; 16 per cent of

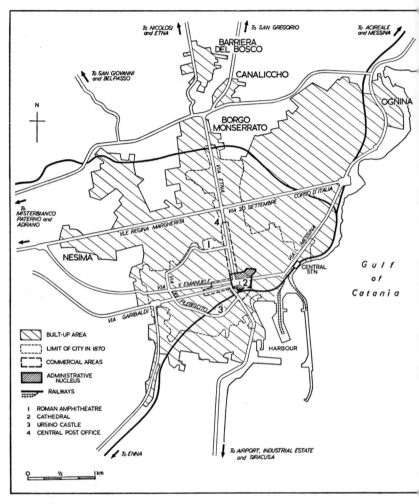

G   Street plan of Catania

the working population is engaged in commerce, the highest percentage of any city in Sicily. Catania's commercial and marketing functions extend far beyond provincial limits over much of the eastern half of the island. Its shops have long been famous for quality furniture, clothes and household goods. The city is second only to Palermo as a cultural centre. The university was founded by Alfonso I of Aragon in 1445, and there are numerous theatres and libraries as well as teaching and research institutes.

The Greek colony of Katane was founded here in 729 BC by Chalchidians from Naxos, attracted no doubt by the fertility of the volcanic soils. The greatest classical prosperity was in the Augustan age, when the city was rebuilt after the ravages of war and an eruption of Etna in 121 BC. An earthquake wrecked the city in 1169, killing 15,000 and, soon after, it was sacked by Frederick II, who built an impressive castle in 1232 to hold down the rebellious population. Only the keep of this castle survived the great lava flow of 1669, which hardened as a solid moat around the wall. Catania's worst disaster was the 1693 earthquake in which 16,000 people, two-thirds of the inhabitants, were killed.

The city's present-day grid-iron plan was laid out around 1700 by the Palermo architect Vaccarini. One favourable result of enforced eighteenth-century urban renewal was that the city was well prepared for its considerable commercial growth. The working-class quarter focusing on the appropriately named Via Plebiscito was agreeably laid out in modest baroque, whilst the finest residential quarters are to the north, around the Giardino Bellini. From the pre-earthquake figure of 24,000, the population grew to 45,000 in 1800, reaching 140,000 by 1900 and 360,000 at the 1961 census. Rapid urban expansion continues on the fringe, especially to the west along the Misterbianco road, eating into the rich vineyards that surround the city, and to the south towards the airport and the new industrial estate. Abrupt changes of level are common in the city and its environs, as almost the whole of Catania is built on the irregular surface of lava flows of various dates, and there are occasional unreclaimed areas of lava surface, such as the Barriera del Bosco.

Siracusa was the island's second Greek colony: founded, according to Thucydides, in 733 BC, one year after Naxos. By the fifth century BC, under first Gelon and then Dionysius, it became the largest city of ancient Greece, with a population of perhaps 200,000. It covered not only the island of Ortygia, but large areas on the mainland (the four quarters known as Achradina, Tyche, Neapolis and Epipolae). Siracusa experienced alternating periods of prosperity and depression under the Greeks. In 212 BC it was taken by the Romans and, although preserved by them as a naval base, the city's importance declined for virtually the next 2,000 years. Brief periods of rebirth took place under Byzantine rule in the ninth century and under the Normans in the eleventh, but the city gradually retreated to its ancient nucleus on Ortygia, leaving Epipolae and the mainland strewn with as vast a collection of classical debris as the Mediterranean world has seen. Expansion back on to the mainland began in the latter half of the nineteenth century. The broad straight streets of the recently built quarters are very different from the cramped layout of Ortygia, although the island remains the nub of civic life. The city grew particularly rapidly after the Italian conquest of Libya between the wars, for Siracusa was well placed to play a strategic role in Italy's expansionist schemes in North Africa. With post-war oil-based industrialisation mushrooming in this part of Sicily, Siracusa has regained its classical position as the island's most dynamic and rapidly developing city. Where once stood the Greek cities of Thrapsos and Megara Hyblea, on the little Magnisi Peninsula and around the Bay of Megara, now rise fine new plants and factories which provide work for upwards of 6,000 of Siracusa's 80,000 inhabitants. To its industrial and commercial functions is added an important agricultural market organisation, specialising in oranges. Siracusa is also a leading tourist centre, with many fine hotels. The National Museum in the beautiful Piazza Duomo, a mixture of medieval and baroque, houses some of the most important Greek exhibits outside Athens.

TRAPANI

Relatively little visited by foreigners and tourists, Trapani is a pleasant place, white and bright under the influence of the sea and the salt works, and thoroughly Sicilian in character. With a population of 77,000, it is now the fifth city in the island, and the largest west of Palermo. Founded as the landing stage for Eryx (Erice), a hilltop town of great classical and medieval importance just inland, Trapani's early history was that of a great port. Being close to Africa made it an important naval settlement during the Carthaginian, Roman, Arab and Spanish periods. The peninsula on which the ancient city was situated is about 2km long by about ½km across and points via a chain of rocks towards the Egadi Islands. The north side of the peninsula faces the open sea and the south the landlocked harbour. On the south side of the harbour is a flat area given over entirely to salt pans. The oldest part of the town, with narrow and irregular streets and many fine if inconspicuous medieval buildings, occupies the central position of the peninsula, covering an area rather less than 1sq km.

Trapani's expansion on to the mainland is fairly recent, provoked by the post-eighteenth-century prosperity of local fishing and agriculture, and the development of industries based on salt and coral. The town suffered heavily from bombing during the last war and most of its approaches are marred by blocks of flats and offices. This modern growth has now carried the city to the foot of Mount Erice. Trapani is the centre of the Sicilian salt industry, and an important producer of wine, tunny and sardines. More recently developed industries include fertilisers, cement and stone working; building stone is quarried round about.

AGRIGENTO

Agrigento crowns a flat-topped ridge 4km in from the south coast. Now one of the smaller provincial capitals, 2,500 years ago this was among the richest and most populous cities of the ancient world. Agrigento was the Greek Akragas, the Roman Agrigentum, and the Arab Karkint; and, until 1927, it was called Girgenti. Founded by colonists from Gela in the sixth century BC, a century later it had over 100,000 inhabitants. The city reached the zenith of its splendour during the wise rule of Theron (488–472 BC). Well placed for trade with the rest of the classical world, Akragas exported wheat, oil, vegetables and wine. Sulphur too was already being produced in the vicinity. Sheep and cattle grazed the fields round about and locally raised horses frequently took the honours at the Pan-Hellenic Games.

In 406 BC, after a long siege, the city fell to Hannibal and the Carthaginians. It was rebuilt but never regained its former glory. In 210 BC it came under the power of Rome. As an emporium for wheat, it enjoyed some prosperity, but quickly declined with the collapse of the empire. Under the Arabs, it flourished again, being ideally situated for trading with North Africa, and prosperity continued into the Norman period, when the town became an important bishopric. In later medieval times the city shrunk to insignificance; in the sixteenth and seventeenth centuries it had fewer than 10,000 inhabitants. Although its present population is 42,000, Agrigento covers less than a quarter of the area of the classical city. The Valley of Temples, probably Sicily's most important tourist site, remains superbly isolated amongst the olive groves and the cacti to the south.

Agrigento today is a poor town in a bleak and eroded countryside: the province has the lowest per capita income of all Italy's ninety provinces. Manufacturing is small-scale; the processing of agricultural products into pasta, sweets and oil, and some small trades like furniture making. The fantastic jumble of old houses, if one ignores the dirt and signs of poverty, is picturesque and interesting, especially in the higher quarters north of Via Atenea, but this pile of insanitary masonry poses a problem for social planners.

RAGUSA

Ragusa, the oil and asphalt boom town of the 1950s, is, like most places in the island's south-east corner, pleasant and surprisingly civilised, with an architectural atmosphere of refined baroque. It is in fact three cities in one.

The old city, called Ragusa Ibla, with narrow irregular streets, is on the site of ancient Hybla Heraea. It sits on a narrow plateau top about 1km from east to west but only 200m wide from north to south. The plateau is bounded on the north by the Cava (ravine) di San Leonardo and to the south by the Cava di Santa Domenica, spanned by the imposing Cappuccini Bridge. To the east, at the foot of the plateau scarp, flows the River Irminio. Although partially destroyed by the 1693 Noto earthquake, Ragusa Ibla contains the town's finest churches, medieval and baroque; the palaces of the landed gentry, and the small peasant houses, many of them hollowed out of the limestone hillside. Much of the building dates from the late seventeenth and early eighteenth centuries. The Piazza San Giovanni, with the eighteenth-century cathedral and most of the important civic offices and shops near by, remains the hub of city life today.

Between the end of the seventeenth century and the beginning of the nineteenth, the city expanded westwards along the road to Comiso and Vittoria to cover a new and larger plateau area. Up to 1926 Ragusa consisted of two separate communes: Ragusa Ibla or Inferiore, with 11,000 inhabitants, and the Città Nuova (New Town) or Superiore, with 44,000. Mussolini united the two communes in preparation for the city's elevation to the status of provincial capital in 1927. The newer sector, about 100m higher than the old town, is connected to it by a long and broad flight of steps. Further expansion westwards and to the south has taken place in the twentieth century; this is the third Ragusa of mostly post-war development.

CALTANISSETTA

Caltanissetta, the one settlement of central Sicily that approaches the status of a city, is situated 600m up the southern slopes of Monte San Giuliano (727m), which some historians have identified as the Greek Nissa. The town's strategic location made it a strong point in the territorial organisation of the Saracens, who called it simply Qalat or castle: the origin of the name Caltanissetta as Qalat-Nissa is thus an unusual mixture of Arab and Greek. Conquered by the Normans in 1086, the town remained modest in size, with fewer than 10,000 inhabitants, until the Spanish period. Caltanissetta's prosperity and rapid growth occurred in the nineteenth and early twentieth centuries as capital of the sulphur industry. It was made a provincial capital in 1818 and became the seat of a diocese in 1844.

Today Caltanissetta (1961 population 52,000) is brash, modern, yet somehow rather sad. Behind the blocks of flats and the wide new roads, lies an unemployment figure of around 30 per cent, due to the running down of the sulphur trade. The remaining baroque, which includes the cathedral, is crumbling and unremarkable. Few tourists come here, despite its notable crag-top Castello di Pietrarossa and the fourteenth-century

Santa Maria degli Angeli church. There are still some traditional industries, particularly the manufacture of sweets, honey and liqueurs (the famous *Amaro Siciliano*).

ENNA

Enna, the 'Navel of Sicily', is at the very centre of the island. Its position 1,000m up in a gap in the Erei Mountains, controlling the main cross-island route along the Dittaino and Salso valleys between Palermo and Catania, has given it continuing importance. It was already a site of settlement in the Siculan period, linked to the myths of Demeter (or Ceres) and the Rape of Persephone. Under the Romans it was Castrum Hennae, and under the Arabs Casr Yani, later translated by the Normans into Castrogiovanni, which it remained until 1927, when Mussolini insisted on the revival of the classical name.

Hidden on a shelf almost invisible from below, Enna's sheer slopes always made it difficult to capture; often it was taken only by treachery. The Arabs, having failed by siege, only succeeded by crawling in through the sewers. The angular Lombard Castle at the eastern end of the plateau, its walls growing out of the sheer rock, is strongly evocative of a past epoch of defensive greatness, but only six of the original twenty towers remain. From this imposing monument, circled by a corniche road, the closely built old town slopes down to the main piazzas of the city. The balustrade of the terrace-like Piazza Belvedere affords remarkable views over the centre of the island. Across the valley rises Enna's mirror image of Calascibetta, only smaller and on a more pointed mountain. In other directions can be seen Piazza Armerina, Mount Etna and the glinting lakes of Pergusa and Pozzillo. Enna's cathedral and nine parish churches exhibit a variety of period styles, notably a peculiar local baroque. At the other end from the castle is Frederick II's tower (Torre Federico), a gaunt white octagonal look-out tower. Enna's open-air theatre claims to be the highest in the world.

In 1927, Enna was made capital of a new province taken from parts of Catania and Caltanissetta. The social elevation of 20 per cent of the working population employed in the newly emergent administrative sector is really the only thing that distinguishes Enna from most other interior hill towns. Forty per cent of the labour force still work in agriculture and mining. Economically it is worse than stagnating. It is the only provincial capital in Italy experiencing a declining resident population: 32,000 in 1921 to 26,000 in 1961.

OTHER TOWNS

Termini Imerese, 35km east of Palermo, midway between the capital and Cefalù, has a port of minor commercial importance. Prehistoric finds in a rock shelter near the citadel date to the last phase of the Upper Palaeolithic. Its mineral waters, which may still be drunk, prescribed great importance for the town under the bath-loving Romans. They called it Thermae Himerenses—waters of Himera; Himera was a nearby Greek colony, today marked by the scanty remains of a Doric temple. There are Roman baths down by the sea, a Roman aqueduct 3km east of the town and the ruins of an amphitheatre. A lively town of some 25,000 people, Termini is divided into an older, upper half and a lower, more spacious modern part. There are five pasta factories, using the fine quality water; two olive oil mills; refineries working sulphur and vegetable oil; an ice plant and a small fish-curing industry. In the last few years there have been much larger industrial developments, in chemicals, electricity generating, and car assembly.

Milazzo, an industrial centre and port at the other end of the north coast from Palermo, is situated at the neck of a long, narrow, rocky peninsula that points a crooked finger toward the

Eolian Isles. Milazzo is the ancient Mylae, founded in about 715 BC by Greeks from nearby Zancle (Messina). Two famous battles, both landmarks in Italian history, took place here. In 260 BC Gaius Duilius won a great naval victory over the Carthaginians which opened the way to Roman control in the Mediterranean. Two thousand years later, in 1860, Garibaldi drove the Bourbon forces into Milazzo Castle, forced them to surrender, and concluded his liberation of Sicily. The huge, partly derelict castle which dominates the town was much enlarged and strengthened by the Spaniards in the sixteenth and early seventeenth centuries. Milazzo's existence and relative prosperity are broadly based: on agriculture, industry, fishing and port trade. South of the town, and along the coast in both directions, stretches the flat, fertile, well-watered Milazzo-Barcellona Plain: 100sq km of intensively cultivated vines, fruits and vegetables. Agricultural prosperity gave rise in the late nineteenth century to oil and flour milling, wine making, fruit preserving, to which were added fish curing and, in 1901, the important sulphuric-acid-based fertiliser plant. With the rapid post-war growth of tourism, over three-quarters of Milazzo's port activity has been to and from the Eolian Islands.

Marsala is at the westernmost point of 'mainland' Sicily. Garibaldi landed his 'Thousand' here to start the Unification of Italy. The site is the ancient city of Lilybaeum, founded by the Carthaginians in 396 BC. Under the Arabs, Marsala became the chief port for African communications. Its name derives from Mars-al-Allah, 'Harbour of God'. Later, its importance declined until the economy of western Sicily was transformed towards the end of the eighteenth century by the diffusion of viticulture and the commercialisation of wine. Marsala saw the setting up of the great Anglo-Sicilian wine houses, many of which still exist today: Woodhouse in 1796, Ingham (1804), Good (1811), Carlet (1814), Lipari (1823) and Florio (1831), and became world famous for its wines. Today there are 200 wine-making establishments employing 20 per cent of the town's work force. Marsala itself has 34,000 inhabitants, but a further 56,000 are scattered in 300 hamlets amongst the vineyards.

Twenty kilometres away lies Mazara del Vallo, also with a population of just over 30,000. The Arabs fortified the town and made it their capital of western Sicily. The port flourished under the Normans when it was in regular contact with Catalonia, the Balearics and Sardinia. Although it too has a wine-making industry, Mazara del Vallo is chiefly known as the most important fishing town in Sicily. This will be noticeable to the visitor in the coloured boats bobbing in the harbour, which is the kilometre-long creek of the River Mazara's estuary; in the nets that cover and drape the quayside; and in the women who work and repair the nets in the dark doorways. The whole place reeks of fish and the sea in the Mediterranean heat, even to the surburbs where curing, processing and packing are carried out.

Three more small town ports along the island's south coast are Sciacca, Licata and Gela. Sciacca is the smallest (population 25,000) but in many ways the most attractive. Viewed from just off the coast, it has a remarkable appearance, for it slopes steeply up from the shore in a great staircase of white and grey buildings sandwiched between slabs of blue in sea and sky. It is a spa (once the Roman Thermae Selinuntiae), a fishing port, and increasingly—for there are good beaches in the neighbourhood—a tourist town, still with a pervading Arab-Norman architectural atmosphere.

Licata, at the estuary of the River Salso, was founded by Phintias of Agrigento in about 280 BC. The present-day town of 40,000 is predominantly industrial, with large works refining sulphur and manufacturing chemicals. Nevertheless, 47 per cent of the working population are employed in the agriculture of olives, vines and cereals. The immediate surroundings are rather flat, but a low vine and olive planted ridge rises to the west. The imposing castle on the eastern end of this ridge dominates the town, which spreads out across the river plain towards the port. As the chief outlet of Sicily's sulphur trade, Licata harbour has been very important in the past, but port usage is much declined now.

The only berth along the flat curving stretch of coast between Licata and the tiny anchorage of Scoglitti is Gela. The busy modern port and the sparkling oil refineries belie the fact that it is a very old place. There was already a settlement on this slightly raised coastal terrace in Siculan times. In the seventh century BC, Gela became a Doric colony; a lone Doric temple column remains. Aeschylus, the poet and playwright, died here in 456 BC, supposedly felled by a tortoise dropped by a passing eagle. Destroyed in 405 BC and again in 282 BC, Gela ceased to exist for over fifteen centuries, but fine remnants of classical Gela can be seen in the Civic Museum at Molino a Vento (the site of the original acropolis) and in the tremendous walls that remain in the sand dunes west of the town. Modern Gela dates from Frederick II's refoundation in 1220. The medieval city repeated its classical function as a collector and exporter of agricultural products from the Gela Plain. After 1957 Gela's economy was transformed by the discovery of oil and it became the fastest growing city in Sicily; the 1961 population of 55,000 was more than double that of 1931. It is now the sixth city of Sicily and the largest of the non-provincial-capital towns.

Many of the larger towns that are not provincial capitals are situated just inland from the south coast. Castelvetrano is a sleepy, dusty town on the edge of the great vine area that stretches eastwards from Marsala. Olives and almonds are also grown in the vicinity. Chiefly a centre for wine and olive oil production, there is also some furniture manufacture. Castelvetrano is where the bandit Giuliano was captured; the unprepossessing courtyard off Via Serafino Mannone where his body lay early one morning has become something of a local sight.

Caltagirone clusters picturesquely around a triple-humped ridge that connects the Erei Mountains to the north-west with the Iblei to the south-east. A surprisingly prosperous town for the interior, with a population of over 35,000, it is half as big again as the provincial capital, Enna. Its prosperity derives not only from a fertile agricultural hinterland but from the traditional ceramics industry, and a small industrial estate down by the railway, with sugar-making, oil-milling and soap factories. In spite of being destroyed by earthquakes in 1542 and 1693, and heavily bombed during the war, Caltagirone is an attractive place, with local coloured stone and tiles and pattern work in the stepped alleyways, rich eighteenth-century baroque façades, and fine views from its piazzas.

Much nearer the coast is Modica, a city of 30,000. Sunk among the hills, most of it is spread between the Janni and the Pizzo dei Pruni streams, which join just below the town to form the River Moticano, whose valley is followed by road and railway to Scicli. Modica was a Sicel foundation, with early names of Motyka and Motyce. During the Norman and subsequent feudal eras it developed rapidly; up until 1702 it was the capital of a *contea*—a sort of county seat. The oldest and most picturesque part of the town clusters in a knot of narrow and twisting alleys around the base of the castle. In past centuries a large number of dwellings were excavated out of the soft limestone of the cliffed valleys. In 1901, when the streams flooded disastrously, many people were trapped and drowned in their troglodyte homes. Subsequently the torrents were channelled underground and the flood victims rehoused in a new quarter. Over 10,000 farmers live in the commune territory outside Modica, whose agricultural markets are the liveliest in Sicily. The farms along the garden-like south coast produce excellent crops of vines, fruits and vegetables. Livestock farm-

Page 107 (*above*) The crater of Mount Etna from the air; (*below*) ski-runs near Etna

Page 108 Vallelunga Pratameno (prov Caltanissetta): a typical interior village. Vallelunga was a baronial foundation of the sixteenth century and has the back-to-back cottages characteristic of such settlements

ing is also important, and the town gives its name to a famous breed of local cattle—the Modicana.

The towns of the Iblean region are remarkably fine for Sicily, but Noto, a baroque city of style and elegance on the fringes of European civilisation, surpasses them all. Ancient Noto arose to the north-west of the present site; the medieval city was heart-shaped and spread across a spur bounded by steep rocky sides. In the seventeenth century the population was 20,000 and chronicles tell of stately houses, sumptuous palaces and churches, beautiful fountains and flourishing industries. This city was completely destroyed by the 1693 Val di Noto earthquake and remains today as a picturesque ruin called Noto Antica. The present town, with a population of 30,000, was built in the early eighteenth century on a site 8km to the south-east, lower down and nearer the sea. It rises symmetrically from the main street up to the monumental churches and public buildings. Below, the workers' quarters are equally tastefully handled. Especially distinctive are the wrought-iron curved Spanish balconies. The limestone weathers to an attractive golden colour particularly suited to baroque decoration, justifying Noto's epithet, the 'city of gold'.

Erice, Cefalù and Taormina are towns of particular touristic importance. Erice sits in an impregnable position on a mountain 750m high, less than 3km from the west coast. Mythologically it is probably the richest site in Sicily. The Greeks worshipped Aphrodite here, and the tradition was continued in the Roman cult of Venus Erycina (Erycina means 'heather-loving'). Eryx was the son of Venus and Butes, an Athenian bee-keeper: the cult of bees and heather runs throughout the legends of Erice. For millennia Mount Eryx has been a landmark for sailors. In 1312 the Aragonese built a look-out tower which also functioned as a crude lighthouse; this was later incorporated into the Chiesa Madre near the Porta Trapani (always the main entrance to the city). Because of numerous steep hairpin bends, the road from Trapani winds for 14km to cover the 4km straight line distance to Erice. A cable car makes a more direct ascent every hour. Basically Erice is a museum city, preserving intact, in spite of an increasing number of tourists, its fine medieval character. The Norman castle, situated at the easternmost, highest point of the mountain, on the site of the Roman temple of Venus Erycina, overlooks a frighteningly precipitous drop. The city walls, cyclopean at their bases, survive intact, a vertical accretion of many periods. Inside lies a knot of medieval streets, narrow cobbled and paved alleys, and many old churches. In winter, when Erice is frequently in the clouds, the inhabitants in their long coats flit about like characters from a Victorian melodrama. But in summer it is gay and thronged with tourists. From whichever point one looks out, a stupendous panorama exists, taking in mountain, plain, sea and sky. Inland is the great burnt golden heart of Sicily. To the west the view stretches from Trapani in the foreground, its white salt pans dazzling, to the north coast of Africa in the distance. At sunset, the sea is on fire and the Egadi Islands become dark ships sailing along the coast, perhaps to Carthage or to Rome. Night does not fall, but rises mysteriously from below.

By contrast, Cefalù, an old fishing town midway along the north coast, nestles at the foot of an enormous rock headland which gives the place a Gibraltar-like appearance. Its Arab-Norman character is evident in the narrow stepped streets where sunlight rarely penetrates; in the public wash place carved out of solid rock, and most of all in its famous cathedral, founded by Roger II in 1131. Some of the old fishermen's houses at the water's edge are raised on arches as protection from storm waves. A climb to the top of the *Rocca* is rewarded by a fine panorama of Sicily's north coast and by the discovery of picturesque medieval ruins enclosing the much earlier Temple of Diana. The town's tourist trade is growing rapidly, capitalising on the fine buildings, unique situation and sandy beaches. There is a French *Club Mediterrané* village at Santa

Lucia 1km west of the town, and new hotels and holiday apartments are being built below the Palermo–Messina main road.

Taormina, on its lofty terrace against a mountain backdrop, is Sicily's most famous holiday resort. Owing to its restricted site, 250m up and 3km in from the coast, the old town has been preserved from tourist development, and hotel building is concentrated along the beaches of Mazzaro, Giardini and Spisone. Founded by Dionysius of Siracusa in 403 BC, Taormina flourished as Tauromenium under the Romans, exporting wine, oil and cereals to the mainland. The Arabs destroyed it in 902, then rebuilt it; and Count Roger took it for the Normans in 1078. Some of its many fine medieval buildings are strikingly embellished in black lava and white pumice. The view from the finely preserved Greek theatre is perhaps the most famous on the island. A gap in the surrounding colonnade frames the diagonal slopes of Etna, snow-clad for much of the year, with the town set amidst its cascading vegetation in the foreground. Early this century Taormina became known as a wintering ground for poets, writers and artists. D. H. Lawrence lived here in the early 1920s, as a plaque in the Via Fontana Vecchia records.

8 AGRICULTURE AND FISHING

SICILIAN agriculture has been described as 'an ugly picture in a frame of gold': the dry poverty-stricken core of the island contrasting vividly with the intensively-cultivated, irrigated coastal periphery. Irrigation, covering 7 per cent of Sicily's area, is almost entirely limited to the more productive coastlands, with special concentration in the Conca d'Oro, the eastern slopes of Etna and the Catania Plain. Easily the most crucial variable in the future development of agriculture, irrigation is particularly important for the citrus orchards, which account for half the irrigated area.

From antiquity, Sicily's has been basically a dry agriculture dominated by the classic Mediterranean crops, wheat, olives and vines. In spite of the dryness of the climate, the mountains and the clay hills, the island has very much an agricultural economy, with over 90 per cent of the total area under productive use and over a third of the population engaged in working the land. Especially in the interior, agricultural practices have changed little; for centuries peasants have trudged out to remote fields to toil the hard earth under a broiling sun. Overall production per hectare and per worker are a third below the Italian average, and farmers' incomes 40 per cent lower.

CEREALS

Cereals have been grown since classical times and are still the most characteristic product, covering nearly a third of the island, the highest proportion of any Italian region. In the province of Enna, 80 per cent of the total land area is given over to wheat alone. The island was one of the chief granaries of the ancient world, and, from as early as the fifth century BC, wheat was exported to Athens, Corinth and Rome. Today there is little left over for export. The historical patterns of land use evolution and overpopulation have progressively relegated cereals to poorer and steeper slopes easily eroded by peasant ploughing. The larger cereal farms generally follow a three-year rotation of pasture-fallow-wheat. Smaller farms include beans (the most important rotation crop), tomatoes, peas, cotton and other crops in their cropping patterns.

The area given over to wheat cultivation seems to have remained remarkably stable, at about 500,000–700,000ha, over the last century. The apex was reached in 1934–8, during Mussolini's 'Battle for Wheat' campaign, when the crop extended over 800,000ha. Since then the area has declined slowly to about 580,000ha. The need is to reduce further still, for Sicilian wheat costs are far above Common Market target prices, but an ideal structure of large, mechanised cereal farms cannot be realised until many more people move off the land.

VINES

Vines probably grew naturally in Sicily. Certainly they have been cultivated for over two and a half millennia, for bunches of grapes are depicted on seventh-century BC coins from the Greek colony of Naxos on the east coast. Sicilian wine became famous in the days of ancient Rome and much was exported to other parts of the empire. In the mid-nineteenth century Sicily produced as much wine as all the rest of Southern Italy, and twice as much as Piedmont, the next largest Italian wine-producing region. Today much of the cheaper low-grade wine is for local consumption, but the sweet, alcoholically strong wines make excellent blending wines, and are sent to Northern

Italy and France to fortify more prestigious products. Marsala is still the most famous Sicilian wine and perhaps the only one to reach true international repute. Other wines remain largely unknown because of their localisation and small scale of production.

In the present century viticulture has expanded to something like its former importance, accounting for 20–25 per cent of the island's agricultural income, and covering 8 per cent of the land area. Apart from Trapani province, where some grapes are also grown for fresh fruit and for raisins, other vine-growing areas include the Palermo region; the north and east coasts, especially around Milazzo and Barcellona; the slopes of Etna, and around Ragusa. Four-fifths of the island of Pantellaria is under vines. Although new vineyards are being planted in the west of the island, further expansion is not encouraged because the European market, especially within the Common Market, is virtually saturated. At present only 8 per cent of Sicilian vineyards are orientated to the production of fresh grapes; but there are great possibilities here, especially along the south coast where the mild climate and early arrival of spring permit very early season production.

CITRUS FRUITS

The express trains from Messina to Palermo and Catania run through a succession of citrus groves and, at blossom time or when the trees are laden with their fruit bright against the dark leaves, the scene from the carriage window is unforgettable. In fact citrus orchards occupy only 3 per cent of the land, but because of the intensity of cultivation and the high value of the crop, citrus fruits comprise a third of the agricultural income. In 1969, 1 million tons of oranges, 700,000 tons of lemons and 150,000 tons of mandarins were produced. The 50,000ha of specialised citrus groves represent two-thirds of the Italian total. Sicily now produces (by weight) 63 per cent of Italian oranges, 92 per cent of Italian lemons and 82 per cent of Italian mandarins.

Bitter oranges and lemons were introduced by the Arabs in the ninth century; sweet oranges came from China in the sixteenth century; and tangerines and mandarins were brought from the Sunda Islands in the nineteenth century. Total numbers of citrus trees increased from 6 to 10 million during the period 1870–90, and their cultivation was fairly widespread even in the interior where today very few citrus groves are to be found. The lemons of Palermo and the oranges of Catania and Siracusa were in demand all over Europe, and beyond. The trade was aimed at a luxury foreign market, less perfect fruit being absorbed by the domestic market or by thriving Calabrian and Sicilian industries producing citric acid and candied fruit. In 1929, according to the *Catasto Agrario*, Sicily had 19 million citrus trees, but the Depression caused trade to fall off due to lack of demand. Technological progress, for example the production by Germany of synthetic citric acid, hit the native processing industries, and to cap it all disease (*malsecco*) decimated large areas of lemon orchards. Especially since the Second World War, Sicily has had to face fierce competition from countries like Spain and Israel which, because of recent planting, do not suffer from the antique structures that now afflict Sicilian citrus farming.

The crucial factor is availability of irrigation water. In traditional areas like the Conca d'Oro, Siracusa, and Messina, water comes from small-scale springs, streams and hand-dug wells; in the more recent plantations in and around the Catania Plain, it comes from larger scale irrigation projects involving dams and motor-pump wells. Lemon groves cover 35 per cent of the citrus area, a much lower proportion than in the past (60 per cent in 1930), due partly to the ravages of *malsecco*, from which oranges are immune. Lemons are grown mainly for export; of the Sicilian total, 30 per cent come from the Palermo area and 25 per cent from around Messina. Growth is limited to elevations of up to 250m, on loose sandy and alluvial soils that heat up quickly in spring. Some forced summer lemons (*verdelli*) are grown in the Conca d'Oro and on the east coast near Catania; otherwise the bulk of the lemon crop is picked during the conventional citrus harvest from November to March. Above the lemon groves, at altitudes of up to 500m and in much the same regions, are the orange plantations. Although hardier, the orange tree requires more water and is often grown in sheltered places to avoid destructive winds. Recent planting of orange groves in the south-east means that 70 per cent of the island's oranges come from the provinces of Catania and Siracusa. Tangerines, mandarins and limes account for less than 10 per cent of citrus cultivation in Sicily.

Despite being by far the largest Common Market citrus producer, Sicily is facing serious difficulties. Whilst new orchards are being planted at a rate which approximates a 'citrus fever', on the other hand, the economy of the citrus crops is approaching a serious structural and commercial crisis. Costs of production are much lower in Israel, where citrus farming is highly mechanised, and in Spain and Morocco where labour is cheaper. Sicilian labour, although in abundant supply, is now heavily unionised and expensive. The island also faces competition from other South Italian regions like Apulia, Lucania and Sardinia where new orange orchards are being planted at lower operating costs. Most Sicilian groves, especially those in the Conca d'Oro, are old; the trees were planted close together to secure highest possible yields, but this prevents mechanisation. Citrus farms are almost all tiny and highly fragmented into separate plots. The average holding is less than 1 hectare.

Another problem is that the quality of Sicilian fruit and the varieties grown are not appreciated outside Italy, especially in West Germany, the Common Market's chief citrus consumer. The main Sicilian varieties exported are the *tarocco*, a thick-skinned orange, and the red-fleshed blood orange. Germany and the other countries of northern Europe have become accustomed to the Israeli thin-skinned, pale-fleshed, pipless varieties like the Jaffa. Marketing of citrus would be more profitable if the whole process of selection, packaging, despatch and sales was the responsibility of a central agency. As it is, there are 400 citrus trading companies in Sicily. An ability to work together in co-operatives is not a characteristic of Sicilian farmers, most of whom are proud individualists, each believing his crop to be better than anyone else's.

OTHER CROPS

Olive trees have a much wider distribution than citrus, being more tolerant of heat, cold and poor soils. They are cultivated up to 1,000m and more, yet are especially dense along the hot dry south coast. Much of the steep north coast is carefully terraced and planted to olives, imparting to the mountain sides a great silver-grey sheen when viewed from a distance. Three-quarters of the trees are grown in orchards mixed with vines and other fruits, or even with arable crops; specialised olive groves account for 120,000ha. Olives contribute up to 10 per cent of agricultural income in Sicily; olive oil is an important cooking ingredient, and about 80 per cent of olives go to make oil (15 per cent of the Italian total). Table olives take the other 20 per cent, an amount which, however, accounts for half the Italian total production. Today, olive culture in Sicily is in something of a state of crisis. Most trees are old and production is falling. The capital costs of grubbing up large old trees and replanting with new saplings, which take several years to mature, represent a step few small farmers are willing or able to take.

Sicily's traditional dry agriculture also includes such tree crops as almonds, hazel-nuts, walnuts, pistacchio nuts and carobs. The almond, whose blossom has graced the early spring of the south coast for thousands of years, is by far the most important of these, covering 96,000ha in specialised orchards and a further 160,000ha in mixed orchards. It is tolerant of most of the soil, altitude and climate conditions that the island has to offer (rising to 1,200m on Etna's slopes), but it flourishes most in the limestone areas of south-east Sicily, with 11,000ha of specialised orchards in the communes of Avola and Noto alone. The cultivation of the other nut trees is very much in decline, but the pistacchio, the nut used in the confectionery industry, grows in a remarkable belt, at about 400–800m level, stretching in an arc round the south-west quadrant of Mount Etna. The plant, with its distinctive leaves and shape, thrives on the raw mineral-rich volcanic soil and is well suited to the extremes of heat and cold characteristic of this altitude and aspect. Bronte is the centre of the pistacchio trade, this commune having 1,400ha of specialised pistacchio cultivation and 2,400ha intercropped.

Apples, pears, peaches, apricots, cherries and similar fruit trees are widely grown in gardens and small orchards, or dotted along field boundaries, mostly for family and local consumption. Only figs are grown for a wider market. In fact, great potential exists for some of these fruits, especially peaches, apples and pears, if only orchard farmers would divert some attention from citrus growing.

Cotton is the most important industrial crop. Introduced by the Arabs, its cultivation has undergone a fluctuating development. The principal cotton growing area has been the plain of Gela, accounting for at least half of Sicilian production. Elsewhere, it can now only be found near Sciacca, and in a few fields around Trapani and in the Plain of Catania. Other industrial crops—flax, tobacco, sugar (cane and beet), peanuts —have all but disappeared in recent years.

Horticultural products—vegetables, small fruits and flowers —although only modestly developed as yet, seem destined to a prosperous future. Tomato cultivation has expanded greatly in recent years, concentrating especially on early and late season varieties. The soils and climate of the extreme south are particularly suited to out of season production, and over half of the island's tomatoes are grown in the Ragusa-Scicli-Vittoria region. About half the Sicilian crop is exported fresh to northern markets; the rest is canned or made into paste and puré. Cultivation of other vegetable crops, always irrigated, is confined for the most part to the immediate hinterlands of the large cities, but new developments are taking place in the Plain of Catania and along the north coast. Market garden crops—artichokes, cauliflowers, early potatoes, egg-plant, melons, fennel, onions, and peas—cover an area of 55,000ha. In the remote southern tip of the island, at Pachino, is what is claimed to be the world's largest hydroponics establishment, growing vegetables and flowers without soil, supplying the roots direct with water and essential minerals. The 'farm', of 55,000sq m, produces tobacco, flowers, tomatoes, strawberries, fennel, egg-plant and carrots. The area around Siracusa is also developing flower growing on a commercial scale. At present Sicily has 500ha of specialised flower gardens, mostly under glass and plastic sheeting. This represents 4 per cent of the Italian total. The production is for ornamental and flowering plants, cut flowers and perfume. The principal varieties grown are chrysanthemums, gladioli, carnations, roses and dahlias.

LIVESTOCK

At one time, before the rise of the large cereal estates and before the growth of population had caused the fragmentation of all non-estate property, the keeping of animals was the principal source of the island's economy. Nowadays livestock farming is poorly developed, contributing only 15 per cent of agricultural income. A few high villages in the northern mountains still live almost entirely from pastoralism: Geraci Siculo at 1,077m, San Mauro Castelverde at 1,050m, Capizzi at 1,139m, and Castel del Lucio at 776m, but generally the upland pastoral economy is everywhere in decline.

Sheep are the most numerous, although numbers have been falling, from 1 million in the 1900s to about ½ million today. Goat numbers were halved during the decade 1958–68. Asses, mules and horses are likewise declining, their functions largely replaced by the scooter and the scooter-lorry—the three-wheeled van much used in rural Italy.

Cattle on the other hand are on the increase, though numbers are very modest compared with other parts of Italy. Forage crops like lucerne are being introduced into the cereals rotation, replacing fallow and beans. Indigenous breeds of cattle are the Ragusana and Modicana, but Friesians and Brown Alpines, generally more productive strains, are being introduced where the grazing and forage are good. Some successful cross-breeds with native stock are reproducing the best qualities of each—high milk productivity and tolerance of heat. The traditional open-air economy is being replaced by winter stalling and more scientifically controlled feeding. Milk production has become much better organised under collection and marketing boards; packaged cows' milk is replacing that from sheep and goats, and the same goes for cheese. In the south-east of the island around Ragusa, enormous pear-shaped cheeses weighing up to 50kg are made for export to emigrant Sicilian communities.

FORESTRY AND FISHING

Like most Mediterranean islands except Corsica, Sicily is very poor in woodland, due in part to soil and climate, both being unfavourable to tree growth, and in part to historical depredations. Today true forests are limited to the northern mountain chain and the middle slopes of Etna. According to recent estimates, forestry contributes only 1 per cent of agricultural income in Sicily. Since 1950, the island's government has pursued a policy of modest reafforestation, mainly for soil conservation and water retention.

With 1,500km of coast (including the minor islands) it is hardly surprising that fishing has been an important activity for centuries. In Sicilian society the 30,000 fishermen are a little world unto themselves, with settlements, customs, a vocabulary and work rhythm entirely their own. Very distinct, for example, are the fishing quarters of the large coastal towns: the *Cala* of Palermo, the old harbourside quarters of Catania and Marsala, and the lines of simple fishermen's houses in the smaller ports. The majority of Sicilian fishermen are very poor. Only about a sixth are employed on large motor fishing boats; the rest go out in small motor-assisted rowing boats, with an average of two men per boat. Some of them are forced to work part-time as boat-hirers and life-savers on the resort beaches, and in agriculture.

Sicily has almost a quarter of Italy's fishermen, landing about a fifth of the country's fish. Half are concentrated in the fishing settlements of the province of Trapani, of which Marzara del Vallo is the most important. Sardines, anchovies, and mackerel are the main catch, and the principal fishing waters are the shallow seas between Sicily and the coasts of Tunisia and Libya, although as much as a third of the total income from fishing comes from molluscs and crustaceans. Swordfish are taken in mid-summer along the Straits of Messina; this is proving an increasingly profitable branch of fishing, thanks to the high prices that the meat commands. The fishermen of the Torre Faro zone catch 70 per cent of the total Italian swordfish. Tunny fishermen live in *tonnare*, small groups of old houses built on the quayside or beach around the tunny traps and only used seasonally from March till June. The principal *tonnare* still existing are: Torretta Granitola and Tre Fontane (south-east of Marzara del Vallo); Favignana, San Cusumano and Bonagia, north of Trapani; Secco, Scopello and others around the Golfo di Castellammare; Trabia near Termini Imerese; Tono, San Giorgio and Oliveri along the north coast near Milazzo; Santa Panagia near Siracusa; and Marzamemi near

Pachino. The tunny trap consists of two vessels and a complex of nets set a certain distance offshore. The crew man the ships in shifts, sleeping in the barrack-like *tonnara* buildings and cooking their own food, often over open fires of driftwood. The climax of the tunny season is the *mattanza* when all the fish are crowded by nets into a restricted area and massacred till the sea is red—a somewhat barbarous practice that has become a minor tourist attraction.

9 LAND REFORM AND AGRARIAN UNREST

THE observant traveller will notice, especially in the interior, small box-like two- or three-roomed cottages dotted about an otherwise deserted countryside. Sometimes these custom-built farmhouses are occupied and surrounded by patches of green-oases of intensive cultivation in a sea of pasture and scrub. More often than not the boxes are uninhabited concrete shells. These are the visible results of Sicily's attempt at land reform, representing respectively success and failure. The attempt to break up the large quasi-feudal estates—a charade typically Sicilian in character—dates from December 1950.

THE AGRARIAN STRUCTURE

The greatest hindrance to the development of agriculture in the island has been the persistence of the latifundia system. The large estates go back to Arab and even Roman times, when lands were distributed to politicians and victorious soldier-leaders, who entrusted their day-to-day operation to managers or agents. Thus was born the pernicious phenomenon of the absentee landlord, a characteristic that persists to this day. The Normans and the Aragonese, fostering feudalism to enable them to rule effectively, consolidated the large estates into a socio-economic institution that persisted with comparatively little modification for seven centuries. In eighteenth-century

Sicily baronial influence was stronger than anywhere else in Europe. The barons owned most of the land but paid few taxes. Generally they cared little for the welfare of the peasants. At the end of the century the landowning aristocracy counted 142 princes, 788 marquises, and 1,500 assorted dukes and barons. About twenty of these landowning families wielded overwhelming political, social and economic power. The various tenure reforms of the eighteenth and nineteenth centuries, ostensibly designed to improve the lot of the peasantry and the efficiency of farming, actually brought about a worsening of conditions. Feudalism was abolished by law in 1812 at the instigation of the British who occupied the island for some years during the Napoleonic period. However, for most peasants the loss of their age-old *usi civici*—the rights to pasture animals, hunt and glean —was disastrous, for they had not the resources to purchase land and were thus reduced to the status of landless labourers. The period to 1860 repeated the tendency. Enclosure and the distribution of ecclesiastical lands similarly favoured the existing landholder rather than the semi-landless peasant. Ten per cent of all rural property was held by the Church; only 7 per cent of this passed into the hands of the peasants. As late as 1876 over 80 per cent of peasants owed allegiance to feudal overlords.

Latifundia are basically of two types. In its simplest form— *latifondo capitalistico*—the estate is managed centrally and run with a number of labourers hired on a daily contract. The main crop is wheat, with sheep pasturage on the fallow, although over parts of the southern interior even this is prevented by the heat and drought of summer. The *braccianti* (the day-labourers) assembled at dawn in the main piazza of the village in the hope that they might be hired by the estate manager for a day's poorly paid labour. If it rained when they got to the estate they were sent home with no pay. Winter was a period of prolonged unemployment when the men hung around in the piazza or in the bars.

The majority of the land, however, is leased or rented out in

Page 125 The way of life: (*above*) Racalmuto (prov Agrigento). Water is a problem in the island, especially in the interior villages. The majority of the poorer homes are without running water, and the people must collect it daily from the public fountain or communal tap; (*left*) Grotte (prov Agrigento). A characteristic Sicilian back street

Page 126 (*above*) Dolci's Palermo. A scene in a back street slum of the island's capital; (*left*) the festive costumes of Piana degli Albanesi. The inhabitants of this town in the mountains south of Palermo remain faithful to their Albanian heritage by wearing their traditional costumes regularly. They continue to speak Albanian and practise the Greek Orthodox rite

much smaller units; this is *latifondo contadino*—the 'peasant latifundium'. In this *gabella* system a whole chain of renting and sub-renting prevailed; the rents, in cash or in kind, getting progressively more burdensome as they descended towards the poverty-stricken peasant. The central figure was the *gabelloto*, an intermediary who leased large blocks of land from the big landowners, splitting it up further and renting it out to peasants in small parcels at extortionate rents and on insecure contracts. The *gabelloti* were the most important and strategic group in the rural economy and social structure. Economically they were parasitic, but wielded enormous power. As land controllers they were able, in the face of increasing population pressure and land hunger, to continually bid up rents. The interest of the *gabelloto*, who was also often a *mafioso*, was in quick profits. Virgin soil, often on steep hillsides, was ploughed up and over-cropped with wheat. No peasant renting land for a one-crop season would plant vines or trees, which take several years to mature, or build cattle stalls, or even fertilise the land, if he knew that he would not be there in succeeding years to reap the benefit. Irrigation was unknown in this sort of system. Peasants paid rents of half or even three-quarters of the crop to the *gabelloto* for the privilege of using scattered scraps of land. The peasant, living far away in his hill-village, thus became 'absentee' too. Because his rented parcel differed in location from one year to the next he could not build a farmhouse, and in any case his income from agriculture was so meagre that it had to be supplemented by the odd jobs that were only available through the social contacts of the village.

Land ownership and control of land were the basic components of social class. Even in the twentieth century the social prestige of leisure and landownership has outstripped the desire for economic growth; it is still said that the social status of a person is determined by the lateness of the hour in the morning at which he appears on his balcony in his pyjamas. As absentee landlords, the *baroni* were not a familiar sight in the village, except in the hunting season. Far more characteristic and dominant in the village life were the *borghesia*. This class was composed principally of *gabelloti*—some of whom, in spite of humble origins, aspired to the class of the aristocracy and took the prefix title of 'Don'—and the doctors, lawyers, clerks and so on. Although the old aristocracy and the rising bourgeoisie (in the form of the *gabelloti*) were in many respects mutually antagonistic, their intentions coincided on one point: the exclusion of the peasants from landownership and the prevention of land reform. The *borghesia* were essentially rentiers fulfilling few of the functions of entrepreneurship, obtaining their livelihood instead from sinecures, high rents and exploitation of the peasants. The peasants, through relationships of patronage and clientelism, were entirely dependent upon the *borghesia* for work opportunities, favours, credit and most of the functions of society.

PRECEPTS TO THE LAND REFORM

After Unification, three factors—population growth, the peasants' increasing self-awareness, and the increase of knowledge on the part of outsiders about what conditions in Sicily were really like—led to efforts to improve the land structure.

In 1876, Franchetti and Sonnino published their classic study of Sicily. The exhaustive peregrinations of these two distinguished Italians enabled them to present an accurate and extremely detailed picture of conditions in the island. The peasants were the most poverty-stricken in Europe; rural illiteracy was almost 100 per cent; crime was profitable and openly protected by the big landowners and the Mafia; in the western part of the island brigandage was rampant. At the same time a parliamentary commission also inquired into conditions in Sicily. The Bonfadini committee's information was derived partly from local nobles who were obviously concerned to screen the truth. While Franchetti and Sonnino pointed to an alarming social crisis demanding prompt and far-reaching action, the official inquiry refused to admit that there was anything more than some general disorder. Ten years later another, much larger, official report was published, edited by Jacini. But few people can have bothered to read the results of these inquiries, and no remedial action on the part of the government resulted. The Sicilian peasants, however, after centuries of downtrodden passivity, were discovering themselves. Strikes by agricultural labourers wrested better wage and tenancy agreements from the landed proprietors. Co-operatives were formed, a most important advance in a land of individualistic and mutually competitive peasants, to administer *latifondi*, cutting out the *gabelloti*. Luigi Don Sturzo, the radical priest of Caltagirone, was instrumental in setting up co-operatives and credit organisations. Emigration too was lessening pressure on land; labour was no longer in such abundant supply and agricultural wages rose by 30 per cent over the period 1906–11. But by the First World War and the rise of Mussolini the emigration flow had all but dried up.

As a result of Mussolini's visits to the island in 1936–8, a new law was passed in 1940. The Sicilian *latifondo* colonisation scheme represented new tendencies towards a more definite land reform approach. It was the first law to point decisively to the immediate colonisation of private latifundia by new scattered settlements, though only eight villages and 2,500 houses were built in the brief period before the war. In 1944, under the communist minister of agriculture Gullo, a law was passed which authorised the occupation and cultivation of uncultivated and waste land by peasant co-operatives. By the spring of 1945, 200,000ha had been taken over by peasants in Sicily, Calabria and Apulia.

In 1947, latifundia were still dominant over two-thirds of the island. In the large area stretching in an arc to the north and east of Caltanissetta and Enna they were more or less the only agrarian structure. Many estates were in the range of 200–

500ha, but holdings of over 1,000ha were common. For the island as a whole less than 1 per cent of the landowners owned half the land, whilst at the other extreme 88 per cent of the landowners—the small semi-landless peasants—possessed between them less than 20 per cent of the land area. In a typical *latifondo* commune, only 10 per cent of the land was worked directly by its owners; over half the land would be owned by a single *barone*, and as many as 90 per cent of the peasants were landless labourers.

THE REFORM LAWS OF 1950 AND THEIR OPERATION

Throughout the late 1940s groups of peasants, some led by priests, some carrying the red flag and singing the *Internationale*, driven basically by hunger but also increasingly by political conviction, continued to occupy *latifondi* illegally. The communists rallied the peasants to the land reform pledge, thus giving the movement an ideological basis. However, the goal that the peasants were striving for was ownership of a small farm—politically one of the most conservative institutions ever developed! They were, therefore, a 'situation' class rather than a revolutionary class psychologically aware of its ideological position. The situation was also critical in southern Italian regions, especially Apulia, Lucania and Calabria. After winning the 1948 Italian elections, the Christian Democrats under De Gasperi planned a broad series of social reforms, the most vital of which was land reform. While discussions were taking place, a group of peasants occupying an estate at Melissa, a mountain town in Calabria, were fired on by the police and three fatalities resulted. To prevent an ugly situation from spreading, legislation was rushed through for the Italian mainland in May 1950.

By this time Sicily had its own regional parliament. The Sicilian reform law, passed on 27 December 1950, is mainly evasionary in character, reflecting the considerable power of the landowners in the regional government. Certain types of culture, such as irrigated land and citrus orchards were exempted from immediate expropriation; instead, landowners had to present plans for the improvement of their land; and no time limits on the whole operation were set. Direct expropriation only concerned owners of over 200ha in the *latifondo* zone, but landowners could appeal to the Court of Justice (and how many judges were also landowners?) and get their quota for expropriation reduced drastically on a mere promise of land improvement, a promise which the Sicilian land reform agency, *Ente per la Riforma Agraria in Sicilia*, ERAS, had no effective power to enforce. One large landowner in the province of Catania, for example, had his expropriable quota reduced from 1,000ha to 70ha.

Peasants eligible for land assignment, being too numerous for the land available, drew lots; the lucky ones received plots of between 3 and 6ha. The slowness with which the reform was carried out enabled the large landowners to divide up their lands into parcels of less than 200ha amongst heirs, and to sell excess land to *gabelloti* and other middle-class agriculturalists. Really unscrupulous landowners, in order to avoid expropriation, forced their landless peasant labourers to buy plots of the estate land, charging extortionate prices and threatening those who did not buy with the prospects of permanent landlessness and no work. When land did pass to the reform agency it was sure to be the worst quality that the landowner possessed. In this way the land expropriated consisted of hundreds of small patches scattered throughout the island, none of it in fertile plain areas. Under strict interpretation of the law, 1,943 properties were liable for expropriation, but such was the 'flexibility' with which the exemption clauses were applied that only a quarter of the land was actually obtained. In 1954, ERAS had published expropriation plans for only half the 150,000ha promised. Only 19,000ha had actually been assigned to beneficiaries, who numbered just 4,000. Although it is publicly claimed that over 450,000ha have now been expropriated, the area actually in possession of the assignees, according to figures issued by ERAS in 1969, is less than 100,000ha (3 per cent of the island's productive area), and beneficiaries number 23,500. Some 4,592 farmhouses and nineteen service hamlets have been built, as well as 533km of roads, 63km of aqueducts and 55km of power lines. The official cost of the land reform is given as £2,000 ($5,600) per assignee. If all the assignees were successfully settled on their holdings and able to live from them, this would not be excessive, but they are not.

An enormous bureaucracy has grown up to carry out the slow and rather ineffective process. To the 6,000 already employed in the regional government, ERAS added another 3,000; 2,000 of whom work in the £533,000 ($1.5 million), eight-storey ERAS headquarters in Palermo. The bureaucracy was built up almost entirely on personal recommendation and patronage, and consists of provincial *borghesia* with little knowledge or interest in the aims of the reform and the welfare of the peasantry; indeed the majority of the agency staff were drawn from the class which by nature opposed the reform. Of the £32 million ($90 million) spent by ERAS in its first eight years of activity, one-third went on 'administrative costs'. The agency had 3,000 employees to administer 15,000 assigned units; one employee for every 20ha of miserably poor land assigned and for every 5 assignees. This prompted one critic to claim that if all the money spent on running the agency was used for land acquisition on the open market, it would have been possible to distribute as much land to the peasants free as they were assigned by the reform!

Another third of the budget went on building farmhouses that for the most part are not lived in. The most notorious example of such waste—about £533,000 ($1.5 million)—is to be found near Francavilla di Sicilia to the north of Etna. Here, at the end of several miles of rough track, amidst the forbiddingly beautiful scenery that surrounds the great volcano, 160 houses grouped in five villages remain completely deserted. The same pattern is repeated in other parts of the island. Borgo Manganaro (near Vicari) is completely deserted; most of the farmhouses and services in the four hamlets near Contessa Entellina are disused; and at Desisa, in north-west Sicily, only seven out of seventy-two houses built by ERAS are permanently inhabited. The farmhouses, containing but two rooms, are far too small for the average large rural family. Many, including those inhabited, already show constructional defects. Those built of prefabricated units are unsuited to the fierce heat of summer. In many cases roads and basic services are lacking; even when such services were provided the houses were often empty and robbed of their fittings.

Numerous studies show that where assignees do attempt to cultivate their plots and live in the new houses, conditions of life are not notably improved. In one sample of 130 assignees, only eighty-four plots were worked directly by the assignees and only 54 beneficiaries declared themselves satisfied. Over half the beneficiaries possessed no animals or farm equipment. The plots provided an average of only sixty days work per year, thus contributing little to improvement of income and living standards. Capparrini, where only a quarter of the farmhouses are occupied all year round, is 40km away from San Giuseppe Iato, the assignees' village of origin. It is so isolated that no post can be delivered. In winter, rainwater can be collected; but in summer water must be fetched in barrels from Roccamena 5km away. Assignees are afraid to go out at night because there are no lights in the hamlet. Yet when the builders built the houses and the road they had light and water laid on from Roccamena; when the builders went so did the wires and pipes. After two years large cracks were appearing in the farmhouse walls. In order to make ends meet most of the assignees have to live six months on the land and six months back in their village of origin doing odd jobs. Cases of successful land reform assignments do exist—at Lentini, for example, where the assignees have planted orange groves; at Petralia Sottana, and in some of the 400 scattered holdings near Gela—but generally the picture is of abandonment and waste.

Only a fifth of the Sicilian land reform plots have been provided with a farmhouse on them; this means that the majority of the assignees must continue to live in their old village residences. This would not be so bad if the assigned units were always accessible from the village, but at Ramacca, Mazzarino and Calascibetta, for example, the plots are as much as 45km, or five hours' travelling time by mule, from the assignees' village. This is one example of the lack of collaboration between the ERAS bureaucracy and the peasants. For those assignees who were provided with farm cottages, ERAS made remarkably little attempt to facilitate the transference of the farm families from their overcrowded villages to the new holdings. The cultural patterns of rural Sicilians are entirely geared to concentrated settlements. Perhaps more than any other folk, they are gregarious by nature. They cannot do without the piazzas, the church and the bars, all of which are missing in dispersed settlement. Although the housing and sanitary standards of the villages' narrow streets and tightly packed hovels leave much to be desired, there is at least electricity, and water from the public fountain, and above all that strong community spirit so characteristic of the Mediterranean village.

Moreover there is the question of security. Although it is certainly true that conditions of safety in the country have improved considerably in recent years, in some parts there is still no question of leaving cattle unguarded in the fields; by day they are carefully watched over and at dusk they are led back to the village. If the Mafia no longer dominates the western rural areas so much as it used to, old traditions die hard. The history of Mafia killings in the Corleone area, for instance, where sixty-two people were shot between 1944 and 1959, prevents most assignees from setting up a farmhouse to live on the land.

LAND REFORM AND AGRARIAN UNREST

The work of ERAS, for all its shortcomings, has been opposed by very strong factors of physical geography and human backwardness. To pass a land reform law is one thing but for that law to function in a land still dominated by *padrone* and the Mafia is quite another. Except in small patches here and there the reform has not basically altered the settlement or cropping patterns of the interior *latifondo*. A further factor is the corruption assumed by the peasants to exist in the land reform apparatus. Many peasants were so spiritually and morally downtrodden that they could not accept that a land reform would actually happen.

What is perhaps most fundamental, however, is that the scale of the work bears so little relationship to the size of the problem. Up to 1957, whilst ERAS struggled to distribute 50,000ha, the peasantry on their own initiative acquired 280,000ha on the open market without any kind of government help. In 1950 Sicily had around 300,000 landless agricultural families. Half of them presented requests for assignment— presumably the rest did not bother because of ignorance or because they had no chance of success; only 68,000 were accepted as valid requests; and a number far smaller again actually received land. There is no doubt that discrimination, often by local priests, who usually supervised the drawing of lots for assignments, took place at both levels, selecting those who had the right to request land, and choosing those who actually got it. At Corleone, for instance, the commune council distribution committee accepted only 871 of the 2,161 applications as being valid, and selected only 152 for assignment. Rather than satisfying peasant demand for land, the most significant sociological result was to heighten feelings of jealousy and class distinction within the peasantry.

It is by now acknowledged that land reform was a primarily

political phenomenon which made an almost negligible contribution to solving the island's economic problems of poverty and unemployment. But things are changing. In 1966 the reform agency became the agricultural development organisation; ERAS became ESA—*Ente di Sviluppo Agricolo.* The policy has now broadened from a half-hearted one of land redistribution and *latifondo* colonisation to a wider programme of irrigation, technical assistance, co-operation, credit and land improvement. Large irrigation projects are under way in several parts of the island. ESA no longer insists on trying doggedly to settle peasants on tiny 3–6ha plots of remote *latifondo,* realising the problem of isolation and the fact that a few hectares of clay and rocks can nowhere near support a farm family. The number of *gabelloti* has declined greatly in recent years. Many have become surprisingly efficient medium-size farmers enjoying the support of government grants and incentives for land improvement. But the older peasants, born into and thoroughly conditioned by the two-class system, will probably never be able to take full advantage of the changing situation. There are still pockets of great poverty and illiteracy, especially in the west-centre. Dolci has shown that even here startling results are possible at the local level. Taking ten villages in the interior *latifondo* part of Palermo province, he established that agricultural improvements eliminating present wasteful practices could provide virtually full employment. But the extension of this approach to the whole of Sicily is unlikely because of official and Mafia opposition and because there is quite simply only one Dolci.

The basic problem of rural Sicily is that there are too many people on the land. Its population is fertile but most of the land is not. A peasant can still be seen pushing a plough that has not basically changed since Roman times; a tragically anachronistic situation in Europe of the 1970s. In some respects, Sicily has not substantially changed since Franchetti and Sonnino's epic inquiry nearly a century ago.

10   THE DELINQUENT SOCIETY

DELINQUENCY in Sicily, or at least those forms of it which have had historical and political significance, can be categorised into three types: the Mafia, banditry, and the *fasci*. Of these the first is the best known, in terms of notoriety, and the most important, permeating at one time or another just about every aspect of the island's economy and society.

ORIGINS OF THE MAFIA

From very early times the feudal baron maintained control over the peasant-labourers of his estates by means of gangs of armed guards, called *compagnie d'armi*. As feudalism was gradually abolished during the nineteenth century, private guards disappeared. With tenancy replacing serfdom new forms of intermediary grew up between peasant and master, chief among these being the *gabelloto*. In the absence of an effective judiciary in the island, these intermediaries, rapidly gaining power through control of the chief economic good, land, were able to establish their own code of law and order. The Sicilian code of honour, *omertà*, based on 2,000 years of foreign rule, considered it dishonourable to have the rights and wrongs of everyday life judged by a non-Sicilian body; law was based on direct and personal revenge, and on a strict public silence of witnesses. Although the roots of the Mafia may lie buried in the fifteenth and sixteenth centuries, when Spanish rule was so incapable of reaching areas of the island outside the main towns, it is not a medieval institution. Its greatest period of glory lies after 1890. The names Mafia and *Onorata Società* (Honoured Society) became current only just over 100 years ago; historians can trace no mention of the word 'mafia' before 1860.

'Mafia' has come to be a term of several nuances. Firstly, it is a state of mind, a general attitude. Used in this adjectival sense, and spelt with a small 'm', it represents the code of behaviour which tends to develop in societies with no effective public order. Sicilians refused to invoke state law in their private quarrels. A Sicilian made himself respected and safe by winning a reputation for toughness and courage. His first recourse if he needed help was to kinsmen, but in dealing with the threatening world of non-kin he needed friends or 'friends of the friends', whose assistance could be called upon by virtue of past service by himself or a kinsman, or some future reciprocal favour. The only obligations recognised were this reciprocal arrangement and the code of honour or *omertà*, which forbade giving information to official authorities. Secondly, 'Mafia' referred to the patronage that governed most relationships in Sicilian society. Its typical form was the interdependent favours, many of them of a feudal nature deriving from the old latifundian society, that flowed to and from the local power-leaders. Such retainership was an expression of the rigid system of social hierarchies, which it in turn tended to reinforce and formalise. In the third sense, the meaning most usually ascribed to the term 'Mafia' is the control of most aspects of the island's life by a system of gangs whose existence, though officially unrecognised and even denied, is known by virtually everyone in Sicily and many beyond.

THE OLD MAFIA IN ITS HEYDAY

The theory and practice of the Old Mafia developed in its most classic form during the period from roughly 1890 to the First World War. Mafia was essentially a 'parallel' system of law and organised power, in fact the only system of effective law in rural Sicily. For the landed aristocracy, and the rural bourgeoisie that gradually replaced the big landowners, it was a means of safeguarding property. For the peasants, it provided some guarantee that traditional obligations would be kept, that the normal degree of oppression would not be exceeded. Also for the peasants, the only chance of socio-economic improvement was through friendship of and patronage by the Mafia. For the middle classes—especially the *gabelloti*—it was a means of gaining and preserving power. And for Sicily as a whole it was a means of self-assertion, of defence against successively the Bourbon, Piedmont and Rome governments. The chief figure, indeed the backbone of the Mafia until recent times, was the *gabelloto*, nearly all of whom were *mafiosi*. Other common members of the Mafia were lawyers, contractors, middlemen; like *gabelloti*, all intermediaries and men of wealth, typical members of the non-productive *borghesia* class. From their central though parasitic position in society such middlemen were able to control transactions in all directions.

The Mafia's activities were strongest in three areas: the latifundia zone of the central part of western Sicily; the irrigated fruit-growing region around Palermo, and the sulphur-mining areas of the south-central part of the island. Outside the four western provinces of Palermo, Trapani, Agrigento and Caltanissetta, Mafia influence tended to be much weaker. In the eastern half of the island society was more open, forward-looking and prosperous. The traders and industrialists of Catania, Siracusa and Messina were aware of the dangers of Mafia involvement; without the scourge of the Mafia, Catania had by about 1900 become the richest city in Sicily, and the murder rate in the province of Caltanissetta was more than ten times that of Siracusa.

The most common forms of Mafia activity were cattle rustling and compulsory protection of crops. *Abigeato*, the theft of livestock—usually cattle, but also sheep, pigs, donkeys and horses—was easy in the interior *latifondo*, devoid of roads and scattered farms. Compulsory guardianship of crops was more common in the rich citrus groves of the Palermo Conca d'Oro, where the farming population lived in concentrated settlements away from their orchards and were thus unable to prevent nocturnal raiding of crops. Mafia protection was thus the only answer. If a farmer thought he could escape Mafia influence, he was liable to find his orange trees, olives or vines cut down or stripped of their fruit just as they were about to yield heavy crops. This was the warning of even more drastic retributions in the future if he did not co-operate and pay for Mafia protection at a determined rate fixed according to his income. If a live-stock owner ignored preliminary Mafia overtures, he was liable to find some of his animals missing; if he was in any doubt as to who was responsible, one animal would be left behind ritually killed. When the farmer agreed to Mafia protection, and few had any choice, he became a member of the Honoured Society, one of the so-called 'friends of the friends'. The pattern was the same in the sulphur mines of the Caltanissetta area. Just as on the estates, labour for the mines was organised by *mafiosi*. Mafia intimidation was directed on the one hand at the miners and, on the other, at the mine owners and managers. If the first group refused to co-operate, they were out of a job; if the second group acted stubbornly, the mines were set on fire.

Other rural activities of the Mafia included credit to farmers and the control of water for irrigation. Irrigation water was the lifeblood of the Conca d'Oro citrus growers and, by the mid-nineteenth century, Mafia monopoly control and a lowering of the water table had imposed a scarcity value on the resource; farmers had to hand over a third of their gross income as pay-ment. *Mafiosi* were able not only to decree who benefited from the Banco di Sicilia's credit distribution but also, by infiltrating the higher echelons of the bank's administration, to amass private fortunes by embezzlement. When the Marquis Notar-bartolo, who was made director of the bank to put straight the financial irregularities, began to tread on *mafiosi* toes, he was first 'warned'—in traditional Mafia fashion—by kidnap and ransom, and then in 1893, when he decided to pass on incriminating information to the government, he was brutally murdered. Typically, the trials of the assassins dragged on for ten years, resulting in final acquittal through 'lack of evidence'.

Towards the end of the nineteenth century the Mafia expanded its activity into every possible field of crime. Syndicates of *mafiosi* sprang up in commerce, industry, transport, gambling and public works. The Mafia built up a fleet of large motorboats to transport stolen cattle overnight to Tunisia. By the turn of the century, the Mafia had become very strong in the larger urban centres of western Sicily, particularly Palermo, Trapani and Agrigento. The organisation probably developed some sort of co-ordination based on Palermo, the chief economic and political centre of western Sicily and the outlet for the agricultural products of Mafia areas. The real organisation of the Mafia, however, was a lateral one based on *cosche*, or groups of families and friends, controlling particular areas and sectors. Each *cosca* would be responsible for a particular estate or group of communes, and specialised in a certain activity like cattle-theft, sale of fruit, the renting of *latifondo* or even the kidnapping of ransomable people. Another, less common, form of grouping was discernable at a higher level, with the *consorteria* consisting of all the *cosche* engaged in the same form of activity. Thus, there was one 'consortium' controlling the citrus plantations, another the Palermo slaughterhouses, another the mines, and so on. Generally the *cosche* and *consorterie* worked as independent units, but most were forced to co-operate with each other occasionally, especially concerning the clandestine movement of stolen livestock across the territories of neighbouring *cosche*. Inevitably, clashes of interest occurred and the various *cosche* often spent their time and energies feuding with each other. A famous example was the feud between the Mafia groups of Bagheria and Monreale, which lasted from 1872 to

1878 and led to dozens of murders on both sides. Pantaleone relates how one man whose relatives had all been killed in the feud decided to tell all to the investigating judge, finishing with the words: 'I shall be killed by the Mafia without a shadow of a doubt, and neither you with all your authority, nor all the police in Italy can save me.' Sure enough, eleven days later his body was found, with a cork stopper placed symbolically in his mouth.

The Mafia had a code of behaviour and a language all of its own, which enabled its members to communicate without others understanding. Standards of dress, bearing, behaviour and talk made *mafiosi* instantly recognisable to those in the know. Mafia language, like the talk of most criminal sects, is full of words with precise and symbolic meanings. A *cosca*, for instance, is an artichoke heart. In the word for being caught by the police—*pizzicatu* (pinched)—there is a parallel with English. Mafia jargon is accompanied by a whole series of gestures of the hands, feet, shoulders, belly and head as well as winks and facial expressions.

The Mafia in its heyday was extremely powerful politically, although the organisation did not always follow a consistent policy line. Initially the Mafia was loosely allied to the left wing, supporting the regional movement of the 1860s. The emergence of the Mafia into a middle-class capitalistic function, however, and the rise of the threat of worker power in the form of the *fasci* and other socialist movements, solidified the Mafia generally on the side of conservatism. Its activity in politics at the local level was concerned with a very effective protection of the chosen candidate and a rigging of elections. The elected candidate thus had an 'obligation' to the local *mafiosi* to help and protect them in any way he could. At the regional and national levels Mafia political policy followed practical rather than ideological considerations. Generally they threw in their lot with the party in power, so as to have as many deputies as possible in Rome. In the case of Nasi, the head of Mafia in Trapani, they even had a cabinet minister in power.

(*above*) A *festa* at Taormina, the popular tourist resort, showing part of a procession of regional costumes; the small Sicilian cart, richly carved and painted, depicts heraldic scenes from the island's turbulent history; (*below*) the *Ballo della Cordella*, a survival of pagan festivals, at Petralia Sottana (prov Palermo)

Page 144 Mondello, a fashionable resort: (*above*) the beach has velvety sand and brilliantly clear water; (*below*) the semi-circular bay overlooked by Monte Pellegrino

It is interesting to reflect on the role of emigration in the development of the Mafia. It was easier for the Mafia to retain its power in a society continually being denuded of its younger and more progressive elements. But some of the emigrants themselves were *mafiosi* or at least 'friends of the friends'. *Mafiosi*, who were in irreparable trouble with the police or whose lives were threatened by internecine strife within the 'brotherhood', could be smuggled out by their friends to America with the aid of the Mafia's private boats. By the 1880s Mafia colonies had sprung up in most large American cities, that of the New Orleans docks being particularly strong. Although the motives of the Sicilian-American 'Black Hand' gangs were more those of pure crime and profit than power and prestige, there were several similarities in methods used. By the early twentieth century there was already some feedback from the United States with the more ruthless methods of racketeering, gambling and gang warfare being introduced into Sicily.

THE NEW MAFIA

Over the last fifty years the Mafia has changed its character considerably. Emigration and the external contacts afforded by two world wars have enlarged the scope of the Mafia's operation, orientating it away from the restricted rural economy of the latifundia. The Mafia made great profits in the First World War from speculation and the illicit sale of goods in wartime shortage, especially foodstuffs. Calogero Vizzini (popularly known as Don Calò), the Mafia boss of Villalba, a hill-village in central Sicily, made a personal fortune out of exploiting wartime shortages.

The Mafia suffered its severest blow ever with the advent of the inter-war fascist regime. Initially Mafia and fascism were not in opposition; there was the same tacit collaboration between the Mafia and the government as had existed in the past, and many *mafiosi* secured prominent positions in the fascist administrative hierarchy. The fascists at first were not all-powerful and needed Mafia help to suppress banditry. Then the Mafia realised the threats to its own autocracy inherent in fascism and that the gradual building up of a police state would inevitably lead to a fundamental clash. Mussolini, after a series of short visits to Sicily, saw for himself the strange all-pervading power of the Mafia in the island, and on one occasion was angered at losing face in a public showing of Mafia protection. The consolidation of totalitarianism enabled Mussolini to build up an all-out attack against this threat to the dictator's prestige. Cesare Mori, an unscrupulous and ruthlessly efficient police inspector, was appointed head of the anti-Mafia drive. In the mountain town of Gangi, which for decades had been ruled by the Mafia, a hundred *mafiosi* were suddenly rounded up and summarily convicted, including the transvestite 'Queen of Gangi', one of the rare female *mafiose*. The same pattern was repeated at all other Mafia centres on the island; mass arrests, torture to extract confessions, connivance of lawyers and judges, wrongful conviction of hundreds of innocent people in a blind effort not to exclude anyone who might be a *mafioso*. Three acknowledged heads of the Mafia were at this time imprisoned; a procedure which would have been unthinkable in the past. They were Don Vito Cascio Ferro, unofficial head of the 'Old' Mafia, who died in prison of a broken heart; Don Calò who was to re-emerge after fascism as the greatest *mafioso* of them all; and Giuseppe Genco Russo, subsequently chief of the Mafia from 1954 to 1964. With the abolition of elections, fascism destroyed the system upon which the Mafia had flourished and had used to get power both locally and in Rome. The Mafia found its functions supplanted by the fascist blackshirts, a body of militia effective in maintaining security in the countryside, even if some of its methods were no less thuggish than those of the Mafia. Mussolini claimed that the Sicilian murder rate had fallen from seventy to three per week, and Mori issued a monthly list of *mafiosi* convicted, some of them condemned to death. Mori's self-glory verged on megalomania; in the end he went too far. Crude accusations against prominent Sicilian parliamentarians brought about his eventual dismissal.

But the roots of the Mafia remained; the organisation could only have been exterminated if the real social problems of the island were tackled. The fascists only dealt with the delinquency problem on the surface. Bandits and *mafiosi* were captured and imprisoned, but the same unwritten law of *omertà* survived as before. The Mafia was not just a group of individuals, it was a way of life. The return to democracy that came about with the collapse of the fascist regime and the gangsterism that followed the allied occupation of the Second World War brought an instant rebirth of the Mafia in both its old form and with new roles.

It is not known exactly how the Mafia emerged after 1943, nor to what extent it was implicated in the allied occupation of the island. That there was a great deal of collusion between newly liberated Mafia chiefs like Vizzini, American gangsters like Lucky Luciano, and the allied commanders themselves, has never been convincingly denied. The inference was that the Americans had allowed gangsters of Sicilian Mafia origin to go ahead of them to pave the way for an easy occupation of the island by arranging things with the Sicilian Mafia. Vito Genovese, one of the most notorious Sicilian-American gangsters, was appointed 'liaison officer', even though he was still wanted by the American police for several crimes including murder. Interpreters, who could speak the Sicilian dialect, and many soldiers of Sicilian parentage in the occupying force, soon fitted back into local kinship networks, since most of them still had relations in the island. The contact fostered by the allies between the Sicilian gangsters of the New World and the old *mafiosi* like Don Calò Vizzini, who was by now recognised as unofficial chief of the Mafia in Sicily, put the *Onorata Società* back on its feet and opened up new fields of criminal activity. The Americans, unwittingly or not, helped the rebirth by appointing Mafia members, as a reward for services rendered, to administrative posts vacated by the anti-fascist purge. Vizzini himself was made mayor of Villalba amid great acclamation, and similar promotions were made all over the *mafioso* part of Sicily. Vizzini and Genovese were old friends. With Genovese installed respectably with allied command at Nola (near Naples) and with Vizzini directing operations from Villalba, a brisk smuggling racket, the biggest black market in all southern Italy, was set up between the two, involving foodstuffs and other goods in short supply. It was during these years that the foundations were laid for the drugs traffic which is now so important a part of Mafia activities.

The Mafia's political allegiances in the post-war years have been with a number of parties. Some *mafiosi* went back to supporting the old pre-fascist right-wing liberals. Most, however, began the immediate post-war period by supporting the separatist movement. Separatism itself was an unlikely marriage of young left-wing intellectuals and old landed notables, all of whom regarded Sicily's decline and problems as dating from union with Italy in 1860. Basically the core of the movement, the landed nobility and the Mafia, looked upon separatism as a blockade to safeguard their interests from rampant north Italian communism which threatened to spread southwards. After about 1946 the Mafia began more seriously to establish links with the coalitionary Christian Democrat Party. This time they backed a winner, for the Christian Democrats have ruled, with varying degrees of strength and effectiveness, since the general election of 1948 and have been consistently reluctant to make an anti-Mafia drive. Throughout this period the Mafia has been able to consolidate its political position by infiltration into the administrative ranks, so that now Mafia power and loyalty to the *Onorata Società* have risen above the party's factional squabbles.

The most important post-war political development has been the rise of socialism and communism, whose parties have been foremost in denouncing the Mafia. Mafia opposition to 'peasant power' was solidified as early as the *fasci* uprising of 1893, and any following the Mafia has had amongst miners and peasants has diminished since then. A famous confrontation, known as the Massacre of Villalba, took place in 1944. The events are recounted in detail by Michele Pantaleone, a young socialist journalist from Villalba, who had already started his crusade against the Mafia in the columns of *Voce Socialista* and the Palermo newspaper, *L'Ora*. As part of the campaign Pantaleone and the Sicilian communist leader, Girolamo Li Causi, decided on the unprecedented step of setting up a meeting in the piazza of Don Calò's native Mafia stronghold. Ignoring typical Mafia warnings from Don Calò, the meeting went ahead. As Li Causi started to speak Vizzini gave the signal for his *mafiosi* thugs to open fire. Li Causi and eighteen onlookers were wounded. Pantaleone escaped unhurt, the wall behind him riddled with bullets. The aggressors were duly charged with the offence but, thanks to the Mafia's capacity for intrigue, the trial dragged on for fourteen years, and resulted in pardon for the accused. Meanwhile Calogero Vizzini died peacefully aged 77 in 1954, ten years after the massacre. His funeral was one of the grandest Sicily has known. The municipal offices were closed for eight days and draped in black crêpe. An epitaph, hung over the church entrance on the day of the funeral, had the effrontery to conclude 'he was an honest man'.

A second bloody manifestation of the Mafia's hostility to socialism was the massacre at Portella delle Ginestre in 1947, when the Mafia prevailed upon Salvatore Giuliano and his bandits to shoot up a crowd of holiday-making peasants from the predominantly socialist town of Piana degli Albanesi. The savage attack on these people enjoying a Labour Day picnic in the fields above their village was aimed at terrorising the peasant movement and creating confusion. There were eleven dead and fifty-six wounded.

In the post-war period Mafia influences have spread to all

sectors of the island's life, and to the realms of international crime. Cattle theft, the traditional Mafia activity in the Corleone area, still occurs sporadically. The nearby Ficuzza wood still provides a hiding place for stolen livestock en route for the Palermo slaughterhouses. But for the most part the Mafia has changed its character in recent years, becoming more involved in big business. There is convincing evidence that the construction industry is now in its hands, not only in Palermo, Agrigento and the towns of western Sicily, but also in Turin and Milan, where emigrant Sicilians provide the vast majority of the labour. *Mafiosi* are active in urban land speculation, and in the control of shops, chain-stores and garages. Typical of the 'New' Mafia, with its close connections with the American underworld, is a ready involvement in drugs, gambling and prostitution. The biggest sources of income now are cigarette contraband and the international drug trade. Throughout the 1950s, until the trick was discovered in 1959, many millions of pounds worth of heroin were distributed from Sicily injected into the island's chief export, oranges. In order to cover up the operation the Mafia propagated the rumour that drugs were sent abroad in sardine tins, and even set up a police discovery of 'planted' drug-filled cans.

Meanwhile Mafia violence continues unabated. Between 1956 and 1960 there were 168 Mafia murders in Sicily, 44 in Palermo alone. In 1947 and again in 1958, the Palermo offices of *L'Ora* were dynamited following publication of anti-Mafia exposés. As recently as May 1971 the chief public prosecutor was gunned down and killed in broad daylight in a Palermo street.

In 1962, the national and regional parliaments agreed to set up the Anti-Mafia Commission to investigate the Mafia and suggest ways of eliminating it. Large numbers of *mafiosi* are now under arrest awaiting trial. In true fascist tradition, many have been sent into *confino*—temporary exile—on the smaller islands off Sicily. Yet the Report of the Anti-Mafia Commission, finally published in 1972, brought few surprises. The evidence accumulated was indeed impressive, but the most controversial parts were withheld from publication. Sicily really needs a fundamental programme of social redemption to break the myth of the Mafia's indestructibility. The Mafia will not be destroyed as long as the law of *omertà* survives, as it still does. There is little doubt that the Mafia remains one of the chief obstacles to Sicily's progress.

BANDITRY

Sicily and southern Italy have long been the scene of intense bandit activity. It was particularly rife in Sicily in the late sixteenth century, corresponding to a period of economic depression and decline in rural living standards. The eighteenth century was another period of violent activity, when the Catinella gang specialised in distributing ransom money to the poor, and so was the period 1860–6. If Mussolini thought he had succeeded in stamping out banditry in Sicily he was mistaken, for it reappeared in a dramatic form in the 1940s. By about 1947 most of the gangs had disbanded, but one group, the Giuliano gang, lived on. The story of Salvatore Giuliano is one of the most romantic Sicily has to tell.

Giuliano was the classic 'social' bandit. He began his career as a victim of injustice; he righted wrongs; he took from the rich to give to the poor; he never killed but in self-defence or revenge; he remained within the community as an honoured citizen; he was admired, helped and supported by his people; he died through treason; his image was one of invulnerability; and he was not the enemy of the king, only of the local oppressors. In addition to these standard bandit qualities Giuliano was young (as are most bandits, for marriage and a family destroy their necessary mobility), being not yet twenty when he started; he was good-looking; he combined ruthlessness against his enemies with ostentatious generosity to the poor; he had considerable powers of leadership; he had great panache; and he had an acute and whimsical sense of publicity. He was certainly not unintelligent for a man of his background and education, but his rudimentary appreciation of the contemporary political scene eventually led to his downfall.

It is essential for the 'noble bandit' to start his compulsory outlawry in a non-criminal fashion. Giuliano shot and killed a policeman when challenged about a sack of flour he was smuggling to his poverty-stricken family in 1943. He took to the hills and caves above Montelepre and formed the nucleus of his gang by freeing his cousin Lombardo and several other men from Monreale prison. Giuliano's early political alliance was with the separatist movement. He drew a famous poster showing himself severing the chain that bound Sicily to Rome, allowing the island to be towed across the Atlantic towards America; he wrote letters to President Truman asking for annexation as the 49th state to the United States; and he was installed as head of the western Sicily section of the separatist army. Attacks were made on police stations, particularly the unfortunately isolated Bellolampo barracks. A considerable portion of the hundred or more police that Giuliano is credited with having killed were dealt with in these early campaigns. Giuliano was never in any way a *mafioso*; but it was clear that as he became more powerful he had to come to terms with the Mafia. In fact, it was the Mafia who skilfully shepherded him into the Separatist Party, who provided him with much of his information about police movements, who exacted an approximate 10-per-cent levy on his financial transactions, especially ransoms, and who, in the end, when it decided that he was getting too dangerous and that it had no further use for him, most probably killed him.

As the American presence and influence declined in Sicily, so the separatists were no longer able to sustain sponsorship of Giuliano. The bandit inclined briefly towards the Monarchists and then to the Christian Democrats, but after 1947 all his political energies, with the Mafia holding the reins as usual, were directed against the communists.

Giuliano had not meanwhile neglected more conventional bandit activities. Early in 1946 he held up the Palermo–Trapani train in broad daylight. He relieved the rich passengers of their money, treated the ladies with great courtesy, and granted a journalist who happened to be travelling on the train a free interview. The many petty spies employed by the police against Giuliano were almost invariably caught and executed; a note was pinned to the body—'So perish all who spy against Giuliano', and thus the Giuliano legend of courage, generosity and infallibility was established. Whilst the government could get nowhere near Giuliano—in spite of a thousand soldiers and police stationed in Montelepre alone—the bandit travelled about almost with impunity, visiting Palermo, his relatives in Montelepre, but always retreating to his honeycomb of caves in the hills. What made things even more annoying for the police was that foreign journalists appeared to be able to visit and talk freely with him. As early as February 1946 a huge reward was placed on Giuliano's head by the police. Soon after, the authorities realised to their horror that if Giuliano were to canvass for political election under the auspices of a legal party, not only would he probably be successful, but also, as a consequence, he would become immune from arrest. Since a convicted felon cannot stand for election, he was hastily tried *in absentia* for the murder of his first policeman, found guilty, and sentenced. As an indirect result of this Giuliano's mother was imprisoned, and was to remain sporadically in and out of prison for the rest of his life. Nothing angered Giuliano more than this, for the relationship between him and his mother was a very close one.

The most enigmatic episode of Giuliano's career was undoubtedly the Portella delle Ginestre massacre on 1 May 1947. The intention, according to Giuliano, was merely to interrupt the proceedings, and to execute Li Causi as an example; the orders had been to fire over the crowd's heads. Whether it was a genuine blunder will probably never be known, but it does seem that if all the gang had been shooting to kill then the casualties should have been much greater than they actually were.

At the beginning of 1949 the number of police stationed in and around Montelepre was nearly 2,000; 400 of the villagers were in Palermo prison, and 2,000 people from the neighbourhood had been rounded up for questioning. Nearly all the relatives of the members of Giuliano's gang were in prison. At the Home Office in Rome, Minister Scelba (a Sicilian incidentally) ordered a Special Committee of Inquiry, which resulted, in August 1949, in the creation of the *Corpo delle Forze per la Repressione di Banditismo in Sicilia* (CFRB)—the Force for the Suppression of Banditry in Sicily. Ugo Luca, the head of CFRB, and his deputy Parenze were able to get some immediate results, largely through collusion with the Mafia. Many of the core-members of Giuliano's gang were captured, and confessed under torture.

At dawn on the 5 July 1950 came the news that shook all Italy and finally exploded the myth of Giuliano's infallibility. The bandit lay dead in a pool of blood in a small courtyard at Castelvetrano, a town some forty miles south-west of Montelepre. The circumstances surrounding Giuliano's death are full of half-truths, claims and counter-claims. The official version was that Parenze had shot Giuliano in a gunfight in the courtyard, but inconsistencies soon became apparent. It seemed more than likely that Giuliano had been killed elsewhere and his body dumped in the courtyard ready for Parenze's shots.

Soon after, Gaspare Pisciotta, cousin and second in command to Giuliano, was captured and sent to Viterbo in central Italy to join the thirty-two whose trial for the Portella delle Ginestre massacre had been interrupted by Giuliano's death. Almost immediately Pisciotta made the staggering announcement that it was he who had killed Giuliano, as he slept, by personal arrangement with Scelba, the Minister of the Interior. At the

Viterbo trial Pisciotta spoke of collusion with the police, as well as with Scelba himself. Pisciotta was given life imprisonment for his bandit crimes. From Palermo's Ucciardone prison he proclaimed that he had many more startling revelations to make over the Giuliano affair, but before he could do so, Pisciotta was murdered, poisoned by strychnine. Clearly the Mafia, which has always been strong within the prison system, was again responsible, for Pisciotta, like Giuliano and Russo (another gang member also poisoned in Ucciardone), knew the names of those who ordered the Portella delle Ginestre massacre. Giuliano's death, at the age of 27, marked the end of an era that can never be repeated in Sicily.

THE FASCI

The *fasci* were, quite simply, groups of peasants, or miners, united for the purposes of self-improvement against the large landowners, the *gabelloti*, and the mine-owners. The movement took the form of meetings, demonstrations and strikes, and developed in the late nineteenth century, especially after 1889. By 1893 there were 163 fully organised *fasci* in Sicily, with another thirty-five being formed. Total membership was in the region of 300,000. In the mines the *fasci* demanded better working conditions, higher wages and more security of contract. In the rural areas they campaigned for division of the latifundia, reform of tenancy contracts and tax reform. Their aims were economic rather than political. The *fascio* swept through Piana degli Albanesi like a tidal wave, recruiting the entire adult male population except for the very few (less than a dozen) families of landowners and *gabelloti*. In dozens of other communes, in Palermo and Trapani provinces especially, the *fasci* organised strikes of agricultural labourers and occupations of the latifundia. In 1893 the Italian Socialist Congress met in Sicily, and in the same year there were congresses of peasants and sulphur-miners. The landowners were worried at this turn of events. Some, like Duke Ferrandina of Caltavuturo, ceded land to the peasants (only for it to be usurped by the *gabelloti*), but most campaigned for repression of the *fasci*, promising future wage increases. Giolitti, the Liberal prime minister, was not to be hoodwinked, and pointed out that strikes were not illegal, especially where they represented genuine grievances. Then Crispi was brought back as prime minister with a policy of martial law. Crispi was a Sicilian, ex-revolutionary and Garibaldian, but like so many islanders who leave for the mainland, he had forgotten the true nature of Sicily's problems. In January 1894, from the opulence and safety of bureaucratic Rome, he sent the navy and 30,000 soldiers to quell the revolt of the *fasci*, claiming that the insurgents were trying to sever Sicily from Italy with the help of Russia and France. The special commission sent with the army acted with implacable severity. All towns and villages with *fasci* were occupied and all organisations, *fasci* or not, were forcibly dissolved. Socialist leaders were arrested, summarily tried, and given severe prison sentences. The total armoury of repression was called upon: banning of newspapers, censorship of postal services, deportation, abolition of right of defence; the flame of popular passion was snuffed out as quickly as it had flared up. The next elections were so rigged as to reinforce the government majority and kill any threat to national unity. Not for nothing was Crispi called the greatest *mafioso* of them all.

But, as with the fascist suppression of banditry and the Mafia, the roots remained to re-emerge in the manifestations of spontaneous and organised peasant political activity that followed each of the world wars. Agricultural strikes for much-needed better conditions still take place, engineered not just by local groups but supported by a socialist, communist and trade union movement of all Italy. The original riotous and millenarian enthusiasm of the *fasci* has given birth to something much more durable.

11   VOLCANOES AND EARTHQUAKES

S ICILIAN history is punctuated by volcanic eruptions and earthquakes, basically due to the fact that the rocks of this geologically young island are still settling down. Etna is the most violent of Sicily's three volcanoes; Stromboli and Vulcano are described on pages 176–8.

MOUNT ETNA

The largest volcano in Europe and one of the greatest in the world, Mount Etna dominates the landscape of eastern Sicily like a distant giant. Bounded on the east by the Ionian Sea, on the north by the Alcantara valley, and on the west and south by the River Simeto, it is 3,290m high; its base covers an area of 1,570sq km, equal to the entire province of Ragusa, and it has a circumference of 210km. Mythology identifies Etna as the forge of Vulcan—earthquakes were his motions, eruptions his breath —and the abode of Cyclops. Ancient navigators regarded it as the highest point on earth. The Arabs called it simply Jebel— the mountain—from which comes its alternative name of Mongibello, 'mountain of mountains'. Etna's cone rises in one long line from sea to summit. The major irregularity of Etna is the Valle del Bove, a sterile abyss 5km wide and 1km deep dotted with minor volcanic vents. This was perhaps the original crater. Altogether some 300 minor cones dot the main volcano's slopes. The original cone only reached about 1,500m (the level of the Valle del Bove), at which level is now a platform representing the ancient crater (called Trifoglio). Above this the volcano is composed of more recent material; the terminal crater probably received its present shape following the great 1669 eruption.

Etna is not only a unique geological formation, it is a distinct human region as well. The volcanic rubbish emitted from time to time weathers within the space of a few centuries into extremely fertile soil. The cultivated lower slopes, especially on the south and east sides, carry one of the densest rural populations in Europe; the villages almost merge into one another and farms become little bigger than gardens. On the west and north sides of the mountain the villages are far fewer in number—Randazzo, Bronte, Adrano and a couple of others—and very much larger in size, over 20,000 inhabitants each. Etna's is a strange, claustrophobic landscape. The soil is black and terraced, or enclosed within cyclopean walls of black lava blocks. The walls may be 2m high and run for several kilometres in an unbroken matrix of tiny airless plots of land. Powerful springs flow from the volcanic ash, providing an abundant supply of irrigation water. The springs of Fiumefreddo ('cold river') are the most powerful in the island, issuing at 2,000 litres per second.

The ascent of Etna is marked by successive climate and vegetation changes. Low down, along the coast and in the Simeto valley around Paternò, lies the citrus belt. At 200–300m orange groves give way to a massive sweep of vineyards that all but encircles the volcano, being interrupted by cereals and pasture on the western side. A large number of Etna's villages are situated in the vineyard zone. Above the vineyards the land use pattern is less regular. There are scattered orchards of pears, peaches and cherries, with pistacchio plantations on the west side between Bronte and Adrano, and pasture and woods higher up. The forest belt at 1,500–2,000m is now much depleted, the original woodland ecology long ago destroyed by timber cutters. Etna wood was sold to Malta and charcoal production was a thriving activity. Bracken and juniper scrub

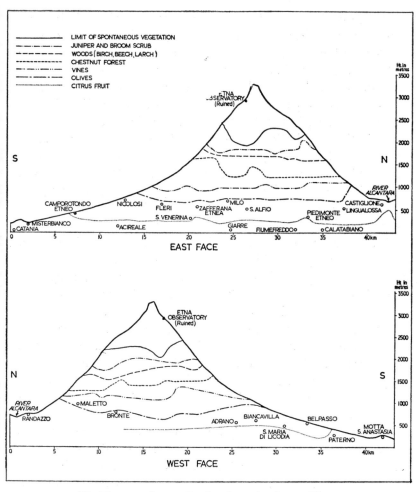

H   Diagram of vegetation bands on the slopes of Etna

are all that is left, and only on the northern side of the great volcano can remnants of the formerly glorious forests of oak, beech and larch be seen, notably above Lingualossa where there is a tourist village built among the trees.

Intermingled with and above the remnants of forest are large expanses of rough pasture. Transhumant pastoralism is now much reduced, but still exists as a nomadic way of life rather rare in the island. The poor quality of the pastures—their steep slopes and frequent damage by volcanic activity—makes them only suitable for sheep, although there were large numbers of goats in the past. Flocks are usually quite large, around 500–2,000, but ownership may be split up amongst various members of a family. The owners of the sheep often combine pastoralism with other agricultural activities linked to ownership of land lower down by the villages. The pasture land itself is usually owned by large landlords, or the Church, and the shepherds rent it for the grazing season. The shepherds lead a wandering life passing up and down the mountain according to weather and season. Generally they are moving upwards between May and June, and descending during September and October. During their sojourns up the mountain they shelter and sleep in *mandare*, groups of small stone and reed huts located at about 1,700m. Their diet consists mainly of *ricotta*, salted sheep's milk cheese.

More common than shepherds on the upper slopes of Etna nowadays are tourists and weekenders. Etna is the playground for all eastern Sicily, and especially for the inhabitants of Catania. On summer Sundays streams of cars follow the 'sea-to-snow' road. The freshness of the mountain air is invigorating after the oppressive heat of Catania and the coastal plains. In 34km the road rises from sea level to 1,880m, from which point a cable car used to operate to the Etna Observatory at 2,942m, only 400m short of the summit. The cable lift and the observatory were destroyed in the 1971 eruption. In late spring it is possible to swim in the Ionian Sea and ski on the upper slopes of Etna an hour or so later. Snow occupies the upper crater from October to June; this was a source of considerable local revenue before the advent of refrigerators. Views from the summit are stupendous, reputedly extending for 250km and on very clear days Malta can be seen.

The zonal pattern of land use up the mountain is frequently interrupted by *sciare*, the tongues of basaltic lava that flow down from the upper vents during Etna's eruptive phases. *Sciare* are a source of both prosperity and destruction for local people. The older channels are transformed by weathering into fertile, mineral-rich soils within a century or so. Gradually the large black masses are colonised by mosses, lichens and then higher-order plants. Prickly pears, often deliberately planted, break up the lava by their powerful stems and roots. Then hardy trees can be planted—almonds, figs, pistacchios—until finally the rock is finely enough powdered to form soil suitable for vines. Thus the lava can often be dated by the stage the vegetational colonisation process has reached. More recent lavas, like the great *sciara* of 1928 that engulfed the village of Mascali, form ugly black stripes in the landscape that interrupt the fertile paradise of green and gold vines and citrus orchards. The black, shrivelled, ropy rivers reach out like tentacles from Etna's crater in all directions; towards Bronte, towards Castiglione diverting the *Circumetnea* railway, towards Riposto, towards Belpasso, towards Zafferana, and most recently towards Fornazzo and S Alfio.

VOLCANIC ERUPTIONS

The first eruptions of Etna, in fact in a 'pre-Etna' phase, were submarine, taking place in a wide bay flanked by the Peloritani, Nebrodi and Iblei Mountains. This early activity was responsible for the pillow lavas of Aci Castello and for the prismatically fractured lavas of the Ciclopi Islands off the coast near Aci Trezza. Etna's eruptive characteristics are midway between those of Vesuvius, whose lava is thick and acidic, erupting infrequently but with great violence (as in the eruption of AD 79 when Pompei was smothered), and those of Stromboli, where eruption is virtually continuous but of low intensity. Etna's activity generally consists of mere exhalations of ashes and smoke, but sometimes intensifies into ejection of lava fragments and bombs, called 'scoriae'. Such effusions occasionally become continuous fountains and are commonly the precursor of a lateral eruption—a lava flow from fractures on the side of the mountain—which is the typical Etnean activity.

Etna is credited, by most sources, with about 100–150 significant eruptions to date. Not more than a dozen or so are attested for the whole of antiquity, and few of them seem to have been heavily destructive. The earliest mentioned took place in about 1500 BC. After four eruptions during the fifth and fourth centuries BC, when the lava reached the coast at Catania (in 477 and 426 BC) and the Alcantara estuary (396 BC), Etna was quiescent until 140 BC, when four violent eruptions occurred within twenty years (141, 135, 126, 122 BC). Three further eruptions followed in 49, 44 and 38 BC. Livy asserts that in 49 BC hot sand was carried as far as Rhegium (Reggio di Calabria), and Pliny says the noise of the 38 BC eruption was heard all over Sicily.

Seven eruptions in a hundred years seems to have exhausted Etna's energies for the next thousand years, apart from minor effusions. The volcano awoke with a vengeance in 1169 when the top part of the cone was blown away. In 1329 lava reached the sea at Acireale and in 1381 it damaged Catania. The worst eruption recorded, in 1669, again altered the configuration of the summit. A tongue of lava 2km wide flowed for over 25km from the central crater, crumbling the walls of Catania, flowing ¾km into the sea and filling up part of the port. Vast areas of the countryside were sterilised. Ashes were carried 100km. The twin cones of Monti Rossi, rising 150m above the side of Etna just west of Nicolosi (destroyed entirely by lava flows), were formed of red sand and ash during the eruption. A whole vine-yard was carried intact like a raft on the lava flow for nearly 1km. The lava took eight years to cool; peasants were able to boil water on it long after the eruption had ceased. The terrified inhabitants of Catania carried the relics of their St Agatha in a procession followed by multitudes of people mortifying themselves with whips. The Earl of Winchelsea stopped at Catania on his way home from his post as ambassador in Constantinople and sent his 'true and exact relation of the late prodigious earthquake and eruption of Mount Aetna' to Charles II. 'In 40 days time,' he wrote, 'it hath destroyed the habitations of 27,000 persons, made two hills of 1,000 paces high apiece and four miles in compass . . . Of 20,000 persons which inhabited Catania, 3,000 did only remain; all their goods are carried away . . . That night which I lay there, it rained ashes all over the city, and ten miles out to sea it troubled my eyes.'

There were sixteen eruptions in the eighteenth century and nineteen in the nineteenth, though none did a great deal of damage. Large scale activity was resumed at the beginning of the present century. The 1910–11 eruption lasted intermittently for over a year, opening 110 new vents including a huge frac-ture on the north-east side of the central crater. The 1928 erup-tion was probably the most serious since 1669. A crater was formed at the new north-east vent and lava poured down in a great tongue to obliterate the village of Mascali, stopping this time just short of the coast at Riposto. At S Alfio, another village threatened during 1928, Monsignor Nicotra announced from the pulpit of the parish church that he would offer his life in exchange for a divine intercession to prevent the lava from entering the village. His request was granted, S Alfio was saved, and four months later he died.

A minor eruption occurred in 1942 and intermittent activity continued till 1947 when it became more violent. During Feb-ruary 1947 volcanic bombs 2–12cm in length were hurled out, some of them landing in the sea. A 7km tongue of lava ½km wide destroyed 40ha of woods and 50ha of cultivated land. A lateral eruption lasting from 25 November 1950 to 2 December 1951 was one of the largest Etna eruptions recorded. Lava flowed from the new north-east vent for 8km and crossed the Lingualossa–Fornazzo upper road in several places before stopping on the brink of a waterfall below Fornazzo. Further violent activity commenced in the mid 1960s, with explosions launching volcanic bombs 200–300m into the air in January 1966.

The most recent eruption took place in 1971. On 5 April two fissures opened 300m below the summit. Somewhat ironically, the lava quickly engulfed the Etna Observatory, the occasional field base of the Catania University Institute of Vulcanology. In May new fissures opened up lower down, at about 1,800m. Lava, issuing at 1,100° C and advancing at about 50m per hour, flowed into the dry valley of the Cubania stream and was channelled down the mountain towards Fornazzo, S Alfio and Macchia, cutting the Lingualossa–Fornazzo road at numerous points. As in 1950–1, when about 150,000 people visited the lava flow, the eruption became a great tourist spectacle. Traffic jammed the narrow roads and refreshment booths and photographers flourished. Thursday 20 May was a local *festa* and 7,000 people watched the lava ooze under and across the road at a bridge. Stallholders selling salami rolls and drinks did record business by day and throughout the night, when the lava emitted an eerie incandescent glow. In less than a month the lava flow reached a point it took 372 days to reach during 1950–1. The inhabitants of Fornazzo, S Alfio and other nearby villages were terrified of what might happen to their homes and their land. Images of local patron saints were paraded in the streets, the bones of the saints were taken up to the lava front, and special masses were held in the churches. Such measures had already been credited with sparing the villages during 1928 and 1950–1. Apart from divine intercession, the possibility of preventing volcanic activity is very remote. At the suggestion of

VOLCANOES AND EARTHQUAKES

Professor Tazieff, the French chairman of the International Institute of Vulcanologists, calls were made for the Italian air force to bomb the erupting fissures to stop the flow or change its course. Tazieff's other suggestion was the construction of an enormous reservoir into which the lava could flow harmlessly. Local vulcanologists of the Catania Institute rejected both ideas as not feasible in the circumstances. As it happened, the river bed channel diverted the lava from the centre of Fornazzo; only a few houses on the northern outskirts were damaged. S Alfio too was spared as the lava turned towards Macchia lower down. Towards the end of May the main lava stream ground to a halt. By early June scientists were convinced that the volcano was lapsing back into quiescence and that the eruption was finished. Damage in the area was nevertheless considerable: 200ha of vineyards and orchards were covered and about fifty buildings, mostly farm cottages, destroyed. Nearly 3km of a tourist road have disappeared. Total damage is estimated at £3 million.

Although the Etna region is one of the richest in Sicily, the people pay dearly for their prosperity, often with their lives. Over a million people have perished on and around the slopes of Etna due to earthquakes and lava flows, though only three have died in the present century—during a minor earthquake in 1952. Etna is a creature of whims; little pattern can be traced in the pattern of the volcano's activity. The science of vulcanology, particularly as applied to the complexities of Etna, is still in its infancy. Until eruptions can be predicted or diverted, people will probably continue to die on these fertile slopes.

EARTHQUAKE DISASTERS

Sicily has witnessed about twenty major earthquakes over the past 2,000 years. The 1693 Val di Noto earthquake was perhaps the greatest natural disaster that has ever befallen the island.

Noto and Modica were entirely destroyed and large parts of Ragusa, Catania and Siracusa reduced to rubble. Horrified observers described how the earth swallowed up rivers, people and houses. Coastal villages were swamped by giant waves. Tens of thousands were made homeless. It is possible that 5 per cent of the island's population died as a result of the upheaval and the spread of disease in its wake. Several hundred minor shocks causing slight or no damage have also occurred. The majority of earthquakes have struck at or near points on the east coast. It was in this area in fact, and in Calabria on the opposite shore, that the scientific study of earthquakes started in 1783.

The most recent disasters are the Western Sicily earthquake of 1968 and the Messina earthquake sixty years earlier. Although Sicily had experienced two serious shocks in the Messina locality, one in 1783 with a death toll of 30,000 and another in 1894 killing 500, there was no immediate precedent for the disaster that struck Messina on 28 December 1908.

The 1908 Messina Earthquake

The main shock took place at 5.23 am, a time when, in winter, few people were up and about. Many were trapped in their houses, crushed in their beds by falling walls and ceilings. The main tremors lasted for only forty seconds, but it was said that the city was utterly destroyed in fifteen seconds. The main shock was of the highest seismological intensity, signifying 'the destruction of all buildings built by man and considerable loss of human life'. In addition to Messina, where 98 per cent of the houses were ruined and forty-nine out of fifty churches thrown down, Reggio di Calabria and most of the coastal villages on both sides of the straits were destroyed. Damage was serious as far north as Pizzo and some houses were wrecked as far away as Catanzaro and Caltanissetta.

The number of dead was probably 100,000–200,000, including about 80,000 in the city of Messina. Disease, including cholera, spread by rats emerging from the broken sewers, added to the disaster. Many survivors seemed to be mentally benumbed, wandering about with a look of stupefied apathy on their faces. One told how he was awakened by a loud rumbling, with the sensation of being lifted up and swayed back and forth in mid air, to be let down again with a jolt. Another, who was in the street at the time of the quake, said that he first heard a low whistling sound in the distance, which gradually grew louder and louder until it became a deafening roar. The earth seemed to move in all directions at once so that it was impossible to stand. Soon after this bewildering blow, which was accompanied by thunder-like rumblings of the earth and the crashing noise of falling buildings, a dead silence spread over the city, only to be broken later by the shrieks and wails of the frightened and injured It was pitch dark, the meagre street lighting extinguished by ruptured gas pipes. A strong south-east wind blew and it was raining.

The day after the earthquake four large Russian ships which had been cruising off Calabria arrived in Messina. Contemporary accounts are full of praise for the courage, hard work and organisational capacity of the Czarist sailors: 'They were angels . . . They did not wait for orders; they saw no danger, but rushed like madmen amongst the crumbling ruins. They worked like Trojans . . . They broke the spell of apathy that bound us.' Soon after, British and German ships arrived to join the human salvage operation, and Americans organised relief aid from nearby Taormina.

The huge doors of Messina's prison were thrown open by the earthquake and some of Italy's most notorious criminals escaped into the town, where they carried out a campaign of robbing, looting and killing. Soldiers shot many of them on sight, but the pillage continued for some days before the thieves were either captured or escaped out of the ruined city.

The earthquake's epicentre was beneath the Straits of Messina. Submarine telegraph cables across the straits and to the Eolian Islands were broken in a number of places. The Messina shore was found to be lowered by up to 1m. Water displaced by the shock reached the coasts in the form of seismic sea waves a few minutes after the main tremors. The waves were generally about 3m high, but reached over 10m at S Alessio. Many houses in coastal districts were washed away by the waves. Both Messina and Reggio harbours were severely damaged. A 15-ton block of concrete from a jetty was shifted 20m from its original position. Messina city contained 112,328 people at the eve of the disaster. For several months after it remained almost completely deserted, with only 3,000 residents in mid 1909.

The bulk of the damage involved crumbling buildings, and this was responsible for the vast majority of the deaths. The brunt of the fatalities was borne by the well-to-do who lived in heavier-built houses and slept in the upper storeys; they had farther to fall, and the heavier masonry crashed on them. The poorer classes lived around the harbour and out on the city's periphery, in single-storey shacks and low buildings, which collapsed quickly with relatively little weight to crush the occupants. Heavy and ornate façades, especially of public offices along the main streets, spared few people on the streets below. The walls of buildings were not structurally bound together, cross beams merely being set in identations in the walls. When the walls moved, the floors, of heavy tiling, simply fell in, the walls collapsing on top of them or falling outwards. Roofs were composed of very heavy tiles which also felled a large number of people. Many streets were narrow, allowing no escape. The disaster emphasised the need to desist from constructing high buildings, to build on anti-seismic 'rafts' of concrete, and to preserve open spaces and wide streets. When reconstructed, the city covered an area three times as great as the old, with working rules of a minimum height of buildings of 10m and a minimum street width of 14m.

VOLCANOES AND EARTHQUAKES

The Western Sicily Earthquake of 1968

The first tremors came on the afternoon of Sunday, 14 January. The worst shock occurred at 3.02 in the morning of the 15th. Tremors continued at frequent intervals until early March, completing a six-week period of terror. The earthquake was accompanied by very cold weather, including some snowfalls. Although the epicentre of the earthquake lay off the coast north of the Egadi Islands, there was relatively little damage to coastal and island settlements. The worst hit villages were those poverty-stricken *latifondo* settlements of the interior. The tragedy of the earthquake was that it struck the poorest part of the island: 280 were killed, 500 seriously injured, and fifty-one villages were affected. Montevago was worst hit. Not one of its 800 dwellings was left standing; 200 of the 3,000 inhabitants perished, most of them women, children and old people, for 70 per cent of Montevago's working males had emigrated. Other badly hit villages were Gibellina, Salaparuta, Santa Margherita Belice, Santa Ninfa, Poggioreale, and Salemi. Large numbers of houses were also affected in Roccamena, Partanna, Menfi, Catalafimi, Contessa Entellina and Castelvetrano. All the settlements involved, being very poor places, were tight agglomerations of badly built peasant homes, unsound structures which collapsed like a pack of cards. Thousands fled into the countryside driven by superstition and the fear of being buried alive in the villages and towns. The normally deserted roads of western Sicily were jammed with people anxious to escape the menace of crumbling masonry.

The earthquake, according to the Italian press at the time, exposed the deficiencies in the authorities' organisational abilities. Money, food, clothing, blankets and tents donated by outsiders took too long to reach the afflicted. The already deficient local services, especially hospitals and transport, were hopelessly inadequate to deal with emergencies. The 50,000 made homeless lived for months in tents and other hastily constructed shelters, buffeted by cold winds, snow and torrential rain. Local Mafia gangs were quick to exploit the situation. Jackal-like they roamed the area, rounding up stray cattle and making offers for land, goods and livestock. Over 15,000 local inhabitants, encouraged by the government with grants of fares, left the disaster area for other parts of Italy and Europe, mostly to join relatives already working there.

12 THE SECONDARY ISLANDS

SICILY is surrounded by a whole constellation of minor islands which form a strange, remote and beautiful world of their own. They include the Eolian group (Lipari, Salina, Vulcano, Stromboli, Panarea, Filicudi, Alicudi) north of Milazzo; Ustica north of Palermo; the Egadi group west of Trapani (Favignana, Marettimo, Levanzo); Pantellaria midway between Sicily and Tunisia; and the Pelagie group (Lampedusa and Linosa) farther down in the Sea of Sicily, southwest of Malta.

THE EOLIAN ISLANDS

The name Eolian (or Aeolian) derives from Aeolus, the legendary god of wind who lived here, keeping his winds in a pigskin bag. The archipelago consists of seven inhabited islands and numerous uninhabited rocky islets. Vulcano, the southernmost island is 20km from Capo Milazzo and Stromboli, the western-most, is 55km from the coast of Calabria.

The Eolian Islands played an important part in Sicilian prehistory; the Eolian Neolithic is divided into four phases running from the middle of the fourth millennium BC to the end of the third. Towards the end of the ninth century BC, Lipari suffered a violently destructive eruption; as a result the Greek colonisation followed as late as 580 BC. Settlement continued throughout Roman and early Christian times, but the islands were virtually depopulated during the Byzantine and Arab periods. A repopulation took place under the Spaniards in the sixteenth

Table 2

POPULATION AND AREA CHARACTERISTICS OF THE
SECONDARY ISLANDS OF SICILY

	Population *1961*	*Area* *sq km*	*Density* *per* *sq km*	*Highest* *point* *metres*
Eolian Islands				
Lipari	9,172	37·3	244	602
Salina	2,737	26·4	102	962
Vulcano	356	20·9	17	500
Stromboli	560	12·2	21	926
Panarea	272	3·4	80	421
Filicudi	447	9·5	47	774
Alicudi	230	5·1	44	675
Ustica	1,262	8·1	156	238
Egadi Islands				
Favignana	4,726	19·9	237	314
Marettimo	1,100	12·3	89	686
Levanzo	307	5·6	54	278
Pantellaria	9,601	83·0	116	836
Pelagie Islands				
Lampedusa	4,387	20·2	217	133
Linosa	424	5·4	79	195

century. The total population of the islands rose from 8,000 in
1400 to 12,000 in 1600 to 18,000 in 1825. The apex was reached
at the 1911 census when the islands contained 20,550 inhabitants. Since then there has been a continuous decline: 17,606
in 1931, 14,749 in 1951 and 13,774 in 1961. Overseas emigration developed strongly in the late nineteenth century, becoming most intense between 1901 and 1914, when over 10,000 left
the Eolian Islands. In recent years 40 per cent of the migratory
flow has been to Australia, with the rest going to Sicily or to
northern Italy. Within the group, people are moving from the
smaller islands to Lipari.

Although the islands now carry a relatively small permanent
resident population, numbers are considerably swollen by an

influx of summer visitors that stretches the islands' services to breaking point. Tourism is probably the only thing that will save the islands from economic stagnation and complete depopulation. Tourist numbers are, however, subject to wide fluctuation (74,404 in 1962; 33,840 in 1964), and will probably not improve until better hotels, sewers, piped water and electricity are provided. Lipari is connected by daily steamer service to Milazzo, this route catering for most of the freight and passenger traffic to and from the islands. A weekly steamship service between Messina and Naples also calls and there is a summer connection to Vibo Valentia in Calabria. A proportion of the boats from Milazzo, Messina and Naples also call at the other islands en route. Hydrofoils ply from Milazzo, Messina, Palermo, Cefalù, Taormina and Catania during the holiday season. Smaller motor boats make frequent connections between the various islands.

Lipari

The largest and most populous of the Eolian Isles, Lipari is the only one to have electricity and a road circuit right round the island. The *Cassa per il Mezzogiorno* has achieved much road improvement work, including a ½km electrically lit tunnel under the headland of Monte Rosa. Lipari is essentially composed of twelve extinct volcanoes in various stages of degradation. The principal peaks are Monte S Angelo (594m) in the very centre of the island; M Chirica (602m) in the north; and two peninsula headlands, M Rosa (239m) between Lipari town and Canneto, and M Guardia (369m) in the south. Post-volcanic activity consists principally of thermal springs; those above the steep west coast at S Calogero are the most famous, their curative powers having been recognised by the Romans. The present-day establishment, containing facilities for mud-baths and sampling the waters, dates from 1867.

The majority of the island's 9,000 inhabitants dwell in the capital town of Lipari, but there is a small coastal village at

Canneto nearby and another at Acquacalda on the north coast. Quattropani and Piano Conte are inland villages widely scattered across a broad, fertile bench about 300m up overlooking the rugged west coast. The lower slopes of the island, especially in the hinterland of Lipari town, are dotted with brightly white-washed cottages of the distinctive Eolian form: rectangular and box-like, fronted by a vine-clad loggia or terrace. As well as the circuit road, all settlements and farms are connected by a network of narrow paths and mule tracks which provide excellent if strenuous walking. The coasts are mostly dramatically cliffed, but there are enchanting little bays with beaches of shingle or black volcanic sand, some only reached by long and tortuous footpaths.

Two volcanic resources, obsidian and pumice, have given Lipari a measure of prosperity. Obsidian, black volcanic glass, when chipped into flakes is sharper than flint; before the use of metals was developed, it was traded not only to Sicily and southern Italy but over much of the Mediterranean. Huge quantities of cores and waste flakes are scattered over the island, especially at Castellaro Vecchio, a Neolithic village devoted to the obsidian trade near Quattropani. Pumice, a light, porous acidic magma effused from M Pelato, is responsible for the strange white landscape north of Canneto. Deep tunnels perforate the 'white mountain', and the pumice is run in trucks on to jetties which discharge straight into the ships.

Lipari town is one of the most attractive little places in the whole of Sicily. The citadel perches on a lava promontory which divides the sea front into two anchorages: the Marina Lunga to the north, stretching round past the colonial-style council offices to M Rosa and followed by the geranium-bordered road to Canneto, and the Marina Corta to the south, used by small fishing boats. The ramparts of the citadel fall sheer to the sea and the tiny quayside. The massive Spanish fortifications, built in 1544 following a terrible sacking by the Barbarian pirate Barbarossa, are built upon foundations which go back to ancient Greek times. Within the citadel are situated the Norman cathedral, the Bishop's Palace (now the Eolian Archaeological Museum), and several other medieval, baroque and later buildings. The old cemetery is informally laid out in a semi-wild public garden of cypresses, prickly pear, trellised roses and wild flowers. The views from the ramparts embrace the town, the surrounding mountains and coast, and some of the other islands. From the castle arches, Lipari's steeply cobbled street runs down to the rest of the town. Fishermens' houses front the two marinas and long red nets clothe the quaysides. Sardine smacks put out nightly from the little 'Peninsula of Purgatory', which juts out from the Marina Corta and contains an old chapel. The local architecture, including that of the town's dozen churches, is, like the Liparians themselves, simple and restrained, yet friendly. The churches are mostly modest baroque, and there is a Spanish influence in the wrought-iron balconies of the larger houses. With its youth hostel in the castle and its range of hotel and inn accommodation, Lipari is the best centre for visiting the other islands.

Salina

Salina is the second largest of the Eolian Isles, both in area and population (2,300 in 1968). Its ancient name Didime, meaning 'twin', referred to the two peaks, M Fossa delle Felci in the east, at 962m the highest mountain in all the minor islands, and M dei Porri (860m) in the west. Between them, bisecting the island in a north-south direction, runs a low saddle, the Valdichiesa, rising to 300m. The only manifestations of volcanic activity are warm vapours east of Malfa and hot gases in the sea off Rinella.

Tourism has developed only slowly. Salina is basically an agricultural island, but much land, especially the higher terraces, has reverted to maquis. Vines and olives still abound, and a good *malvasia* wine is produced. The slopes of the Fossa delle Felci and of the ridge that extends from the summit towards the

175

north are being reforested. The main areas of settlement are: Pollara, isolated on the west coast; Malfa, Valdichiesa, Leni and Rinella, running north to south along the central saddle; Capo on the north coast; and S Marina Salina and Lingua on the east coast. They are organised into three communes based on the three largest villages, S Marina Salina (the chief landing place), Malfa and Leni. A surfaced road extends along the east coast and along the north, with a branch southwards from Malfa to Rinella following the central valley.

Vulcano

As its name implies, Vulcano contains several volcanic craters. Gran Cratere rises to 391m and hangs claustrophobically over the landing stage. The southern part of the island is occupied by 'Vulcano Vecchio' or 'Piano', an old crater much denuded and modified into an upland area of pasture and reafforestation. Its highest point is M Aria at 500m. To the north of Gran Cratere lies the smaller cone of Vulcanello; almost circular, with an elevation of 123m and a diameter of 1·3km, Vulcanello is a perfect miniature volcano. Once an individual island, it is now connected to Vulcano by an ash isthmus less than 1m high. Gran Cratere has erupted fairly frequently, the last severe eruption occurring in 1888. The cyclical pattern of activity would predict another eruption about now. Sulphurous gases are emitted from yellow, sulphur-encrusted vents, both near the summit and around its base. In fact the whole island reeks of sulphur. Fumaroles occur on the beach and just below sea-level, warming the sea water considerably. The thermally heated sea water and the associated mud-baths are visited by tourists and the ailing for their curative properties.

The threat of volcanic activity has limited the populaton and development of the island. It has never contained more than about 400 people. Present-day settlement is limited to clusters of houses and holiday cabins around Porto Ponente and Porto

Levante in the north, and scattered farms around the Gelso-M Aria area in the south.

Stromboli

The island of Stromboli, nicknamed the 'lighthouse of the Mediterranean', represents the emergent third of a volcano, the base of which lies 2km below sea-level. The summit is formed of two crests, 918m and 926m high, separated by a valley 300m wide and 120m deep. Most of the volcanic activity takes place to the north-west of the summit from a crateric plain at 700m dotted with cones and vents. Eruptions are mild and more or less continuous. Most of the eruptive material rolls down a wide channel known as the Sciara del Fuoco into the sea, which steams as the red hot matter enters it. Occasionally, however, activity becomes paroxysmal. Recent explosive eruptions occurred in 1822, 1882, 1891, 1907, 1915, 1919, 1930 and 1954. From the north-east of the island a narrow submarine shelf extends offshore to the islet of Strombolicchio, which rises vertically out of the sea like a great castellated tower. A lava monolith, Strombolicchio has a rock-cut stairway to a terrace and a lighthouse on the summit.

The village of Stromboli is composed of three contiguous hamlets of scattered houses (Piscità, Ficogrande, Scari). Two splendid churches, S Bartolo and S Vincenzo, rather out of character with the charmingly modest houses, divide the agglomeration ecclesiastically into two parishes. The simple Eolian architecture, white, cubic and austere, contrasts pleasantly with ebony black beaches and the dark green of the luxuriant vegetation. Sloping up from the coast in a series of terraces, the land is mostly under vines and olives, with a wide range of scattered fruit trees. Individual plots, many of them abandoned, are divided by walls of black lava or hedges of cacti. The only other settlement is Ginostra, a small village of a few people, and there are a handful of houses at Leni, both on the south-west coast facing Panarea. The majority of the houses on Stromboli

L

are abandoned to ruin or locked up by emigrants until an eventual return for retirement. Between Stromboli and Ginostra there is only a little-used rocky path over the volcano, and the walk takes five hours. Contact between the two sides of the island is mostly by boat, although there is an overland telephone wire.

The path to the summit passes through a pleasantly varied landscape. Vineyards and gardens near sea-level give way to derelict olive groves, above which an area of giant bamboo grasses is traversed. Blackberries and bracken lie above this, succeeded only by mosses and lichens on increasingly immature soils. The last few hundred metres are composed of sterile volcanic matter in shades of grey and black. The air is full of volcanic vapours, and only the hardiest of walkers completes the three-hour climb without some discomfort. Many visitors make the ascent at night (a guide is necessary) for the fiery nocturnal performances of the volcano are a sight unique in Europe.

There is no quay to accommodate the Messina–Naples boat which has to anchor offshore while small boats ferry the passengers across to the beach—either Ficogrande or Scari, depending on direction of wind. When the sea is too rough, passengers must continue to Lipari (or to Naples if coming from Messina!) and await a return boat when conditions are smoother. Nevertheless Stromboli receives a strong summer influx of visitors, including geologists and vulcanologists, but generally only younger people are attracted by the spartan life.

Panarea

Panarea, the smallest and perhaps most attractive of the seven inhabited Eolian Islands, lies directly between Lipari and Stromboli. A large submarine bank extends to the east and north-east, breaking the surface in a number of rocky islets. The largest of these, and the farthest away, is Basiluzzo, where there are remains of a Roman villa with traces of mosaics, and a submerged Roman boathouse.

The backbone of Panarea is formed by a rocky ridge culminating in the Pizzo del Corvo (421m). This ridge drops suddenly to the rugged and deserted west coast; on the eastern, settled side it falls more gradually in terraces. The volcanic tuffs and lavas weather into good soils and in places the island has a fertile appearance. Most of the eastern side is under vines, olives, cereals and grass, with flights of terraces reaching over 300m. Settlement, in the three tiny hamlets of S Pietro, Ditella and Drautto, is scattered, with square whitewashed houses set amongst giant boulders, olive trees and small gardens girt with prickly pear. Each house has its water cistern, though there is one well of potable water. The 1961 population was 272, much smaller than in the past (790 in 1911), and the church is now in ruins. On a cliffed promontory (Punto Milazzese) at the southern tip of the island a dramatically situated Bronze Age village, with thirty-three oval huts, has been excavated. The village dates back to the fourteenth century BC and from it the Eolian Middle Bronze Age, termed the Milazzese Culture after the site, has been reconstructed.

Filicudi

Filicudi is an oval-shaped island consisting of four extinct volcanoes, with a small appendage connected by a low, narrow isthmus. It rises regularly and steeply to its highest point of Fossa delle Felci (774m) in the north-central part. The other peaks are La Montagnola (383m) and Il Torrione (278m), both to the south, and the peninsular peak of Capo Graziano (174m) in the south-east, linked by an isthmus $\frac{1}{2}$km wide and 20m high. There is no good landing place throughout the 13km of rugged and cliffed coastline. Punto Perciato on the west side has a fine natural arch, and to the south of this is a large marine cavern, the Grotta del Bue Marino (The Seal's Cave). A large number of rocky islets grace this west coast, among them La Canna, a narrow obelisk 70m high. Anchorage offshore is obtained north of the Capo Graziano isthmus at Filicudi Porto and on the south coast at Pecorini a Mare.

A dozen oval huts, built of stone and thatch, have been excavated on the summit of Capo Graziano, together with associated burial places on the south slopes. The Early Bronze Age settlement yielded pottery of early Mycenean type going back to the sixteenth century BC. This period represented the first reflowering of the Eolian civilisation after the Copper Age decline which succeeded the prosperous Neolithic. The Capo Graziano culture, evident too in archaeological sites on other islands, resulted from the island's strategic importance on trade routes between Crete (the Minoan civilisation) and Greece (Mid and Late Helladic, or Mycenean), and the western Mediterranean (as far, in fact, as Cornwall).

Present-day settlement is mostly confined to the south-east parts of the island, in the hamlets of Val di Chiesa, Rocca di Ciauli, Filicudi Porto, Canale and Pecorini. Groups of cottages at Seccagni, in the north-west, and at Zucco Grande near the north-east coast are now mostly abandoned. Tourism probably represents the only possible economic salvation for Filicudi (1961 population 447); 4,750 tourists came in 1959, but the number has since fallen back to around 2,000 per year. There are two small hotels, at Filicudi Porto and Pecorini, but in rough weather the island is cut off.

Alicudi

Alicudi, the westernmost and most isolated of the group, is a simple cone rising steeply from sea-level. The highest point is Filo dell'Arpa (675m). The western and northern coasts especially are craggy and precipitous; many of the cliffs are overhanging and pierced with caves. Alicudi's ancient name of Ericusa referred to the heather which covered much of the island. Today the western part is uninhabited, while the eastern half is terraced and dotted with the hundred or so cottages whose 230 inhabitants derive a precarious living from agriculture, fishing, a few tourists, and emigrant remittances.

THE SECONDARY ISLANDS

USTICA

The solitary island of Ustica is the much eroded crater of a long extinct volcano, now weathered to a series of hills, the highest of which reaches 238m. The coasts are rocky, though nowhere highly cliffed. The principal anchorage is the Cala S Marina, a cove below the main village settlement of Ustica, but the Palermo steamship, which makes the three-hour trip every day in summer, must off-load its passengers into smaller boats at the entrance of the bay. Farming and fishing provide a livelihood for the 1,000 or so islanders. Much land is abandoned; rather less than half the island is now under cultivation.

Formerly Ustica was a place of banishment for criminals, *mafiosi* and political enemies of the state. With such a large exile colony surviving into the 1950s, tourism has been discouraged. Only a few hundred devotees of small islands come here for the peace and quiet, and for the excellent underwater fishing. A couple of hotels have been built, but the accommodation otherwise remains simple.

THE EGADI ISLANDS

The group consists of three main islands and a number of uninhabited islets and rocks, which together cover an area of 33sq km. The detachment of the archipelago from the mainland of western Sicily took place only in late prehistoric times. The former land bridge is now represented by a submarine bank less than 100 fathoms deep, which breaks the surface in the uninhabited islets of Formica, Maraone and Stagnone. Buildings on Formica are used seasonally by the fishermen.

The islands are basically composed of porous limestones, with crystalline layers on top. Only Favignana has much cultivable lowland, with two plains of tufa (shelly limestone) deposits. Everywhere the soils are extremely porous. A major pine afforestation project is in operation on the islands' upper slopes, otherwise the only woodland vegetation is maquis. Anchorages abound around the indented coasts, and tunny fishing is a major activity: the harvest of the sea thus compensates for the aridity of the soil. All the islands are connected daily to Trapani by a combination of steamship and hydrofoil services.

Favignana

By far the largest and most important island of the group, Favignana is dominated by Montagna Grossa (314m) whose bare slopes contain a number of prehistoric caves. All but a few hundred of the 4,700 population live in the port of Favignana, on the north coast; the rest are in widely scattered cottages on the plains at the eastern and western ends of the island, connected by a network of untarred tracks. Cereals and vines are grown and a few livestock kept. Fishing is the main economic activity, Favignana being the biggest tunny centre in Sicily. A large canning factory on the western shore of the port provides seasonal work for about 200 people. The other industrial resource is white tufa stone, quarried and exported as a building stone. Tourism is making some impact on the economy with a 1,000-bed villa complex under construction, but there are only two hotels. The Sicilian Institute for Industrial Finance has produced an ambitious study which would make the island the centre of a western Sicily industrial complex, with chemical and metallurgical industries based on the importing and refining of North African oil. There is also a project to build a bridge between Favignana and Sicily via the islet of Stagnone.

Levanzo

A rugged limestone ridge traverses the small pear-shaped island from north to south, rising to 278m at the Pizzo del Monaco. Poor pasture supports a few stock and there are vines and cereals on the restricted gentler slopes. The island has no water supply apart from cisterns. Most of the 300 inhabitants live in the fishing village of Levanzo in the south above a cove, where there is an inn. In 1949 Palaeolithic cave paintings were discovered in the Grotta della Cala dei Genovesi, a limestone cave in the cliffs about 4km west of Levanzo village. The earliest, Upper Palaeolithic in age, are vividly naturalistic, incised figures of deer, oxen, horses, the dwarf elephant and other quaternary beasts. Particularly expressive is a picture of a doe turning its head. These animals could not have existed in such a small island environment; the drawings prove that Levanzo was then part of the Sicilian land mass. A second group of figures are far more schematical, stiff and painted solid in black or red; they are probably later, perhaps early Neolithic.

Marettimo

The square houses and lack of vegetation, particularly trees, give the island and its main settlement, also called Marettimo, an African appearance. Shaped like a parallelogram, the island is the most mountainous of the group, rising to 686m in M Falcone. Some springs of fresh water occur, and it is the only one of the Sicilian minor islands not dependent upon tankers for water supply. As elsewhere in the Egadi Islands, fishing and tourism are linked. The tourists—700 annually—lodge with the fishermen, there being no hotels. Apart from seeking solitude, they come for the underwater fishing and to explore the marine caves around the island's dramatic coasts.

PANTELLARIA

Pantellaria, the ancient Phoenician Cossyra, is strategically placed in the Sea of Sicily 70km from Cape Mustafà in Tunisia and 100km from Sicily. It is linked to Sicily by the steamer that makes the round trip from Trapani to Porto Empedocle twice a week in each direction (also calling, on the stretch between Pantellaria and Porto Empedocle, at Lampedusa and Linosa), and by an air service to Palermo (journey time half an hour).

183

Pantellaria is entirely volcanic in origin. The highest point is the complex extinct crater of Magna Grande (836m) and there are several smaller cones, called *cuddie*. The oldest lavas, which outcrop mainly south-west of M Gibelè (700m) and in coastal areas, are dense and massive. The slopes of Magna Grande and M Gelkhamar (289m) and the recent lava flows of Khagiar, Gelfiser and Cuttinar are of obsidian. In contrast, other parts of the island are covered by a soft pumice in the form of a pale yellow dust. There is one crater lake (L Bugeber or Bagno dell'Acqua) surrounded by salt encrustations and hot springs, but the water is too brackish for use. It is possible that Pantellaria may actually only be dormant, for there were submarine eruptions, accompanied by earth tremors, in 1831 and 1891.

The coasts are mostly cliffed, except in the north where Pantellaria town clusters round the only real harbour. The port is exposed to all winds between west and north-east and access is often difficult in bad weather. Most of the island is cultivated, and scattered with farm cottages or loose groups of simple, cubic, one-roomed houses, in appearance much like the villages of nearby North Africa. The soil is very fertile, but water is scarce and quickly used up by the sponge-like ground. The only springs are thermal, all of them over 50° C. Rainwater is collected in cisterns and there are wells in the north; additional water is brought in by tanker. With 9,600 people living on only 83sq km, agriculture is extremely intensive. Vines are widespread; table grapes, raisins and some good, sweet wine being exported. Other crops include cereals and various fruits and vegetables. Goats and other livestock are kept, and there is some rearing of a special hardy breed of donkey.

There are traces of Neolithic villages on the west coast at La Mursia, 3km south of Pantellaria town. The ramparts surrounding the village are of obsidian blocks and reach 7m in height. South of La Mursia are the mysterious *sesi*, the round or eliptical tower tombs of these Neolithic people, built of rough volcanic blocks. Fifty-seven have been traced; the largest of those visible is Sese Grande, 7m high and a prominent land-mark. Under the Romans Pantellaria functioned as a place of banishment, and today there is a prison in the Norman castle. Many of the present place names are strongly Arabic in character. Because of its strategic position in the narrow passage dividing east and west Mediterranean, Mussolini fortified the island, using rocks, caves and even *sesi* as gun emplacements. There is a large airfield inland, 3km south-east of Pantellaria town. Mussolini also built a good road network, including the fine *strada perimetrale*, which keeps as near as possible to the cliff tops. Pantellaria town has not yet fully recovered from the heavy air bombardment of June 1943.

THE PELAGIE ISLANDS

Lost midway between Europe and Africa, these islands are some of the most primitive and isolated in Europe. The group consists of Lampedusa, the principal island, with Linosa 45km to the north, and the uninhabited islet of Lampione, 17km to the west. A steamship service connects the islands twice weekly with Trapani (via Pantellaria) and Porto Empedocle. For the visitor, the comfort of these ships, with their luxury cabins, bars, lounges and restaurants, is in stark contrast to the primitive conditions awaiting him on the islands.

Lampedusa

Lampedusa, western Europe's most southerly point, is nearer to Africa than to Sicily. The scenery is one of low, whitish limestone hills, formed for the most part of bare rock. The highest point (only 133m) is M Albero del Sole in the north-west corner; from this ridge the land slopes gently south-eastwards. The valley bottoms, filled in with soil washed from the rock by the occasional shower, are cultivated with vines and cereals. Much of the coast is rocky and cliffed, but in the east and south are a number of inlets, the largest of which houses the main settlement, Lampedusa village. Fishing, chiefly for sardines, but also for sponges and coral, occupies most of the working population. Near the village are prehistoric hut foundations, Punic tombs and Roman buildings. In 1553, under Spanish domination, a thousand slaves were taken from the island's population. The owning family of the island, dating from 1436, and Don Giovanni de Caro, Baron of Montechiaro, received the title of 'prince' in 1661. It was one of the descendants of this ruling family, Giuseppe Tomasi di Lampedusa, who wrote the world famous historical novel *The Leopard* in 1955-6.

Linosa

Linosa is entirely volcanic in origin and composed of four cones: M Vulcano (195 m), M Rosso (186m), M di Ponente (107m) and M Bandiera (102m). The coast is jaggedly rocky with cliffs of up to 90m and a few beaches of black sand. A few dozen colour-washed houses constitute Linosa village, on the southern slope of M Bandiera, about ¼km from the south coast. Paths connect the village with landing stages at Scalo Vecchio on the south coast and at Scalo Vittorio Emanuele on the west. The flatter parts of the island are cultivated or used for grazing. About 250 cattle are kept and exported live for slaughter and consumption on Lampedusa. Caves in the hills, once lived in, are now used as stalls or as stores for home-made wine. There is no port, no electricity and no piped water. One refrigerator run on liquid gas is used for summer tourists.

BIBLIOGRAPHY

The literature on Sicily is extremely voluminous. This bibliography therefore lists the major sources and indicates useful lines of approach to further reading. There is a fair amount of material in English, especially on topics such as history and archaeology, and in French and German; but the majority is, of course, in Italian. The bibliography roughly follows the topic sequence of the book.

The best general bibliography of literature on Sicily is:
DI MAGGIO, M. T. *Sicilia (Collana di Bibliografie Geografiche delle Regioni Italiane Vol 4)* (Faenza, 1962; supplement 1965)

Other bibliographies include:
BONASERA, F. *Fonti per lo Studio Geografico della Sicilia 1861–1960* (Palermo, 1968)
CUPERTINO, E. *Regione Siciliana: Bibliografia 1943–53* (Palermo, 1954)
EVOLA, N. D. *Bibliografia Siciliana 1938–1953* (Palermo, 1954)

The two best geographical and general reference books on the island are:
PECORA, A. *Sicilia (Le Regioni d'Italia Vol 17)* (Turin, 1968)
ROCHEFORT, R. *Le Travail en Sicile: Étude de Géographie Sociale* (Paris, 1961)

Other good general works on the island are:
AGLIANÒ, S. *Questa Sicilia* (Milan, 1950)
ARENA, P. *La Sicilia nella sua Storia e nei suoi Problemi* (Palermo, 1949)
CUMIN, G. *La Sicilia: Profilo Geografico-Economico* (Catania, 1944)
D'AGOSTINO ORSINI, P. *Sicilia Regione* (Rome, 1951)
GUERCIO, F. M. *Sicily: The Garden of the Mediterranean* (1968)

BIBLIOGRAPHY

LEVI, C. *Words are Stones; Impressions of Sicily* (1959)
MILONE, F. *Sicilia: La Natura e l'Uomo* (Turin, 1960)
POLLASTRI, F. *Sicilia* (Palermo, 1948–9, 3 vols)
SCROFANI, S. *Sicilia e Mezzogiorno* (Bologna, 1967)
SYLOS-LABINI, P. ed. *Problemi dell'Economia Siciliana* (Milan, 1966)
TOURING CLUB ITALIANO. *Sicilia* (Milan, 1968)

Following 1700 a large number of early travellers, including Dryden, Brydone, Swinburne and Goethe, visited the island; their books are reviewed in:

CIACCIO, C. 'La Sicilia nel XVIII attraverso la Descrizione delle Guide e dei Viaggiatori', *Annali di Ricerche e Studi di Geografia*, 19 no 2 (1963), 45–104

A selection of the even more numerous twentieth-century guides is as follows:

CAICO, L. *Sicilian Ways and Days* (1910)
CRONIN, V. *The Golden Honeycomb* (1954)
KININMONTH, C. *The Travellers' Guide to Sicily* (1972)
OLIVIER, L. *En Sicile: Guide du Savant et du Touriste* (Paris, 1910)
QUENNELL, P. *Spring in Sicily* (1952)
SEBILLEAU, P. *Sicily* (1968)
SLADEN, D. *In Sicily* (1901, 2 vols)

Several thousands of geological references will be found in two bibliographies:

FLORIDIA, G. B. *Bibliografia Geologico-Mineraria della Sicilia* (Palermo, 1950; supplement 1956)
STRAMONDO, A. *Sicilia (Bibliografia Geologica d'Italia Vol 8)* (Naples, 1962)

The two principal single works on Sicilian geology are:

ALLYSON, A. *Guida alle Escursioni della 57ª Riunione della Società Geologica Italiana in Sicilia* (Palermo, 1953)
BALDACCI, L. *Descrizione Geologica dell'Isola di Sicilia* (Rome, 1886)

The most complete survey of the island's hydrology is:

PERRONE, E. *I Corsi d'Acqua della Sicilia* (Rome, 1909)

Other studies of individual rivers and lakes are listed in Di Maggio, 92–103.

On *frane* and *fiumare* see:

CRINÒ, S. 'Frane Siciliane', *L'Universo*, 1 no 5–6 (1920), 335–49; 2 no 6 (1921), 421–66

SPERANZA, F. 'Le Fiumare del Versante sud-orientale dei Peloritani', *Annali della Facoltà di Economia e Commercio dell'Università di Catania*, 10 (1964), 5–32

On climate there is no standard work; *see* the several minor studies listed in Di Maggio, 83–90.

There are a number of weighty nineteenth-century Latin studies on vegetation:

GUSSONE, G. *Florae Siculae Synopsis* (Naples, 1842–5, 2 vols)

LOJACONO-POJERO, M. *Flora Sicula* (Palermo, 1888–1909, 5 vols)

TORNABENE, F. *Flora Sicula* (Catania, 1837)

More recent works include:

BRUNO, F., DI MARTINO, A. & BONOMO, R. 'Le Piante Officinali Spontanee della Sicilia e dell'Archipelago delle Pelagie', *Lavori dell'Istituto Botanico e Giardino Coloniale di Palermo*, 17 (1960), 131–521

FREI, M. *Die Gliederung der sizilienischen Flora und ihre Stellung im Mittelmeergebeit* (Zurich, 1938)

MOLINIER, R. & R. 'Observations sur la Végétation Littorale de l'Italie Occidentale et de la Sicile', *Archivie Botanique*, 31 (1955), 129–61

On settlement geography *see*:

ALMAGIÀ, R. 'Distribuzione della Popolazione in Sicilia secondo la Costituzione del Suolo', *Rivista Geografica Italiana*, 14 no 1 (1907), 1–14

CRINÒ, S. 'I Centri Doppi in Sicilia', *L'Universo*, 3 (1922), 165–78, 221–39, 311–17, 369–94

FLORIDIA, E. *La Distribuzione della Popolazione in Sicilia: Variazioni e Tendenze del Cinquantennio 1911–1961* (Rome, 1964)

MONHEIM, R. 'Die Agrostadt im Siedlungsgefüge Mittelsiziliens: Untersucht am Beispiel Gangi', *Bonner Geographische Abhandlungen*, 41 (1969), 1–196

MORI, A. 'La Distribuzione della Popolazione in Sicilia e le sue Variazioni negli Ultimi Quattro Secoli', *Memorie Geografiche*, 36 (1918), 127–314

——. 'Sulla Formazione di Nuovi Centri Abitati in Sicilia negli Ultimi Quattro Secoli', *Rivista Geografica Italiana*, 27 no 9–12 (1920), 149–77

PECORA, A. 'Insediamento e Dimora Rurale nella Regione degli

BIBLIOGRAPHY

Iblei', *Quaderni di Geografia Umana per la Sicilia e la Calabria*, 4 (1960), 1–102

Toschi, U. 'Questioni di Morfologia Urbana nella Sicilia Ionica', *Rivista Geografica Italiana*, 43 no 1 (1936), 1–28

Tudisco, M. 'L'Insediamento Umano nella Piana di Catania', *Rivista Geografica Italiana*, 43 no 2 (1936), 181–201

Valussi, G. *La Casa Rurale nella Sicilia Occidentale (Ricerche sulle Dimore Rurali in Italia Vol 24)* (Florence, 1968)

The history and prehistory of Sicily has recently been covered in a masterly joint work:

Finley, M. I. & Mack Smith, D. *A History of Sicily* (1968, 3 vols)

Anyone interested in further reading should consult their extensive bibliographic sections, and the volumes of four journals devoted to Sicilian history: *Kokalos* for archaeology; *Archivio Storico Siciliano* the main historical periodical; and, for more local history, *Archivio Storico per la Sicilia Orientale* and *Archivio Storico Messinese*.

The basic works on archaeology are:

Bernabò Brea, L. *Sicily before the Greeks* (1966)

Guido, M. *Sicily: An Archaeological Guide* (1967)

Pareti, L. *Sicilia Antica* (Palermo, 1959)

The following are some of the most important and more recent historical works:

Amari, M. *Storia dei Musulmani di Sicilia* (Florence, 1872; republished Catania, 1930–9, 3 vols)

Freeman, E. A. *History of Sicily* (Oxford, 1891–4, 4 vols)

Lowe, A. *The Barrier and the Bridge: Historic Sicily* (1972)

Norwich, J. J. *The Normans in the South 1016–1130* (1967)

——. *The Kingdom in the Sun 1130–1194* (1970)

Peri, I. *Studi e Problemi di Storia Siciliana* (Florence, 1959)

Scaturro, I. *Storia di Sicilia* (Rome, 1950, 2 vols)

On art and architecture *see*:

Demus, O. *The Mosaics of Norman Sicily* (1950)

Epifanio, L. *L'Architettura Rustica in Sicilia* (Palermo, 1939)

Page, B. *Arte e Civiltà della Sicilia Antica* (Rome 1936–49, 4 vols)

Schwartz, H. M. *Sicily* (1956)

On the Sicilian way of life *see*:

BIBLIOGRAPHY

GALTUNG, J. *Members of Two Worlds: Development in Three Villages in Sicily* (Oslo, 1970)

MAXWELL, G. *The Ten Pains of Death* (1959)

OCCHIPINTI, M. *Una Donna di Ragusa* (Florence, 1957)

SCIORTINO-GUGINO, G. *Coscienza Collettiva e Giudizio Individuale nella Cultura Contadina* (Palermo, 1960)

WEBER, K. E. *Materialen zur Sociologie Siziliens* (Heidelberg, 1966)

Guercio has a lot of material on Sicilian society, customs and traditions, as well as a good guide to literary works (including Pirandello, Verga, Capuana, Brancati, Vittorini, Quasimodo, Martoglio, Sciascia). On the contemporary political scene there is:

PALAZZOLI, C. *L'Ambiente Insulare e i suoi Problemi: Sicilia e Sardegna* (Palermo, 1966)

Mention should be made of Sicily's greatest novel:

DI LAMPEDUSA, G. *The Leopard* (1958)

On folklore the main source is:

PITRÈ, G. *Biblioteca delle Tradizioni Popolari* (Milan and Florence 1871–1923, 25 vols; part republished Florence, 1939, 4 vols)

See also the volumes of *Annali del Museo Pitrè* and:

BRANDON-ALBINI, M. *Sicile Secrète* (Paris, 1960)

BUTTITTA, A. *Cultura Figurativa Popolare in Sicilia* (Palermo, 1961)

CAPITÒ, G. *Il Carretto Siciliano* (Milan, 1923)

LI GOTTI, E. *Il Teatro dei Pupi* (Florence, 1957)

LO PRESTI, S. *I Pupi* (Catania, 1927)

——. *Il Carretto* (Palermo, 1959)

POIGNANT, R. 'Paladins, Puppets and Painted Carts in Sicily', *Geographical Magazine*, 34 no 6 (1961), 337–53

RUBINO, B. & COCCHIARO, G. *Usi e Costumi, Novelle e Poesie del Popolo Siciliano* (Palermo, 1924)

TUCCI, G. 'Il Carretto Siciliano', *L'Universo*, 46 no 5 (1966), 735–60

On the Albanians in Sicily:

BONASERA, F. 'Le Colonie Albanesi in Sicilia', *Atti del 19° Congresso Geografico Italiano (Como)*, 3 (1965), 197–218

PETROTTA, S. *Albanesi di Sicilia* (Tirana, 1941; republished Palermo, 1966)

BIBLIOGRAPHY

On poverty and unemployment:

BIGNARDI, F. *Inoccupazione, Occupazione e Disoccupazione in Sicilia* (Palermo, 1953)

PETREGNAMI, G. 'Sul Problema delle Aree Arretrate: Aspetti Igenico-Sanitari della Sicilia', *Annali del Mezzogiorno*, 4 (1964), 85–149

SCHIFANI, C. *Redditi e Consumi nella Agricoltura Siciliana* (Palermo, 1960)

SYLOS-LABINI, P. 'Precarious Employment in Sicily', *International Labour Review*, 89 no 3 (1964), 268–85

Among the many works on emigration *see*:

ARCURI DI MARCO, L. 'L'Emigrazione Siciliana all'Estero nel Cinquantennio 1876–1925', *Annali della Facoltà di Economia e Commercio dell'Università di Palermo*, 3 no 2 (1949), 11–72

BACARELLA, A. & DRAGO, P. 'L'Emigrazione da Raffadali e Realmonte', *Quaderni di Sociologia Rurale*, 2 no 3 (1962), 80–94

CHIRONI, G. 'L'Emigrazione da Campofiorito', *Quaderni di Sociologia Rurale*, 2 no 3 (1962), 63–79

CRONIN, C. *The Sting of Change: Sicilians in Sicily and Australia* (Chicago, 1970)

CUSIMANO, G. & SPRINI, G. *Orientamenti e Motivazioni delle Correnti Migratorie Siciliane* (Palermo, 1966)

PANTALEONE, M. 'L'Emigrazione dalla Provincia di Caltanissetta', *Cronache Meridionali*, 5 no 5 (1958), 213–17

RENDA F. *L'Emigrazione in Sicilia* (Palermo, 1963)

ROCHEFORT, R. 'L'Emigration en Amerique, avant 1918, dans une Bourgade Sicilienne', *Quaderni di Geografia Umana per la Sicilia e la Calabria*, 3 (1958), 123–35

SIMETI, A. 'L'Emigrazione da Alcamo', *Quaderni di Sociologia Rurale*, 2 no 3 (1962), 95–109

The main works of Danilo Dolci are:

DOLCI, D. *Inchiesta a Palermo* (1956) published in English as *To Feed the Hungry* (1959) and in paperback as *Poverty in Sicily* (1966)
——. *Conversazioni* (Milan, 1962)
——. *Waste* (1963)
——. *The Man who Plays Alone* (1969)

Works about Dolci include:

CAPITANI, A. *Rivoluzione Aperta* (Florence, 1956)

——. *Danilo Dolci* (Milan, 1958)
MANGIONE, J. *A Passion for Sicilians: The World around Danilo Dolci* (New York, 1968)
McNEISH, J. *Fire under the Ashes* (1965)
STEINMANN, J. *Tout le Monde en Parle: Pour ou Contre Danilo Dolci?* (Paris, 1959)
WATJEN, E. *Danilo Dolci: seine Person, seine Arbeit* (Cologne, 1961)

On industry and industrial development:
BELLANCA, A. *L'Industria Marmifera nella Provincia di Trapani* (Trapani, 1963)
BORDIERI, F. *Il Petrolio di Gela* (Rome, 1966)
CAPPELLANI, S. *L'Artigianato in Sicilia* (Catania, 1958)
FASINO, M. *Sicilia e Industrializzazione* (Palermo, 1960)
LOJACONO, V. *Aspetti Fondamentali dello Sviluppo della Sicilia dal 1861 al 1965* (Palermo, 1967)
MANFREDINI-GASPARETTO, M. L. 'L'Industria Zolfifera Siciliana', *L'Universo*, 44 (1964), 703–20, 841–64, 1103–26
MORELLO, G. *L'Industrializzazione della Provincia di Siracusa* (Bologna, 1962)
MOUNTJOY, A. B. 'Planning and Industrial Developments in Eastern Sicily', *Geography*, 55 no 4 (1970), 441–4
PARLATO, V., MAZZARINO, M. & PEGGIO, E. *Industrializzazione e Sottosviluppo: Il Progresso Tecnologico in una Provincia del Mezzogiorno (Siracusa)* (Turin, 1960)
PECORA, A. 'Nuovi Orizzonti nella Industria Siciliana: Interpretazioni Geografiche', *Atti Academia Pontaniani*, 10 (1961), 1–42.
RENDA, F. *Inchiesta nelle Miniere* (Palermo, 1959)
RIVA, A. 'Un Nuovo Paesaggio Geografico: La Cimosa Costiera Industrializzata di Augusta', *L'Universo*, 42 no 4 (1962), 617–43
ROCCA, F. & URBANI, L. *Studio sulla Localizzazione della Industria in Sicilia* (Caltanissetta, 1962)
ROCHEFORT, R. 'Le Pétrole en Sicile', *Annales de Géographie*, 69 no 371 (1960), 22–33
RUOCCO, D. 'Le Saline della Sicilia', *Memorie di Geografia Economica*, 10 no 8 (1958), 5–243
SANTIAPIGHI, S. & VACCARO, G. *Augusta: Industrializzazione in Sicilia* (Palermo, 1962)
STEIN, N. 'Die Industrialisierung an der Südostküste Siziliens', *Die Erde*, 102 no 2–3 (1971), 180–207
VÖCHTING, F. *L'Industrializzazione in Sicilia* (Palermo, 1963)

M

BIBLIOGRAPHY

On trade and commerce:
ARCURI DI MARCO, L., SAIBENE, C., PICCARDI, S. & PECORA, A. 'I
Porti della Sicilia', *Memorie di Geografia Economica*, 10 no 19 (1961),
1–258
D'ARRIGO, A. *I Porti della Sicilia* (Palermo, 1965)
RIPARBELLI, A. 'Aspetti Economico-Tecnici del Commercio con
l'Estero della Regione Siciliana', *Annali della Facoltà di Economia e
Commercio dell'Università di Catania*, 1 (1955), 113–85

On tourism *see*:
LA LOGGIA, G. *Indagine sul Turismo in Sicilia* (Caltanissetta, 1965)
MASTRORILLI, F. *Prospettive e Problemi Turistici Interessanti la Sicilia*
(Palermo, 1965)

For material on transport and communications on Sicily *see*:
BARBERA, C. & DI FALCO, F. *Strade di Sicilia* (Palermo, 1965)
GIUFFRIDA, R. *Lo Stato e le Ferrovie in Sicilia 1860–1895* (Caltanissetta,
1967)
KALLA-BISHOP, P. M. *Mediterranean Island Railways* (Newton Abbot,
1970), 13–92
MIRABELLA, F. 'Il Traffico sullo Stretto di Messina', *Studi di Geo-
grafia Economica*, 1 (1964), 1–62

The following are some of the most important and accessible
references on individual towns and cities:
ANFOSSI, A., TALAMO, M. & INDOVINA, F. *Ragusa: Comunità in
Transizione* (Turin, 1959)
BOSCARINO, S. *Vicende Urbanistiche di Catania* (Catania, 1966)
CALANDRA, A. 'Lo Sviluppo Urbano Problema di Fondo di Messina
dal 1908 ad Oggi', *Cronache Messinesi*, 1 (1957), 1–19
CARACCIOLO, E. 'Ambienti Edilizi della Città sul Monte Erice',
Archivio Storico Siciliano, 3 no 4 (1950–1), 183–258
CAVALLERI, G. *La Popolazione della Città di Catania attraverso il
Tempo* (Catania, 1948)
DI GIOVANNI, V. *La Topografia Antica di Palermo dal Secolo X al
Secolo XV* (Palermo, 1889–90, 2 vols)
FORNARO, A. 'Milazzo Studio di Geografia Urbana', *Quaderni di
Geografia Umana per la Sicilia e la Calabria*, 1 (1956), 14–50
GUIDO, M. *Syracuse* (1958)
HUTTON, E. *Cities of Sicily* (1926)

BIBLIOGRAPHY

MAGGIORE-PERNI, F. *Topografia e Popolazione della Città di Palermo* (Palermo, 1869)

MARCELLINO, V. 'Sulle Piante Topografiche della Città di Palermo', *Archivio Storico Siciliano*, 3 no 2 (1948), 199–223

MORELLO, G. *Petrolio e Sud: Inchiesta a Ragusa* (Milan, 1959)

——. *Aspetti Socioeconomici della Comunità de Gela* (Palermo, 1960)

PARDI, G. 'Storia Demografica della Città di Palermo', *Nuova Rivista Storica*, 3 (1919), 180–208, 601–31

——. *Storia Demografica della Città di Messina* (Rome, 1921)

PERI, I. 'Girgenti Porto del Sale e del Grano', *Studi in Onore di Amintore Fanfani*, vol 1, 619–40 (Milan, 1962)

PISANI, N. *Noto Città d'Oro* (Siracusa, 1953)

PITRÈ, G. *La Vita in Palermo Cento e Più Anni Fa* (Palermo, 1904; reprinted Florence, 1944–50, 2 vols)

SCATURRO, I. *Storia della Città di Siracusa* (Naples, 1925–6, 2 vols)

VILLA, P. *Storia della Vita Urbanistica di Palermo* (Palermo, 1941)

Four excellent studies on Sicilian agriculture and land use are:

MILONE, F. *Memoria Illustrativa della Carta della Utilizzazione del Suolo di Sicilia* (Rome, 1959)

POLLASTRI, F. *Notizie e Commenti Ecologici di Agricoltura Siciliana* (Palermo, 1948–9, 3 vols)

PRESTIANNI, N. *L'Economia Agraria della Sicilia* (Palermo, 1946)

SCROFANI, S. *Sicilia: Utilizzazione del Suolo* (Palermo, 1967)

A selection of shorter studies on individual crops and sectors of agriculture:

CAPPELLANI, S. 'Il Regresso della Tabacchicoltura Siciliana', *Annali della Facoltà di Economia e Commercio dell'Università di Catania*, 3 (1957), 263–96

DONIA, A. 'La Produzione ed il Consumo di Carne in Sicilia', *Annali della Facoltà di Economia e Commercio dell'Università di Palermo*, 21 (1967), 47–90, 115–57

——. 'Di una Azienda Idroponica Siciliana', *Annali della Facoltà di Economia e Commercio dell'Università di Palermo*, 23 no 1 (1969), 1–20

FORMICA, C. 'L'Esportazione dalla Sicilia dei Prodotti Ortofrutticoli', *Bollettino della Società Geografica Italiana*, 105 no 10–12 (1968), 561–86

FOTI, S. 'Le Coltivazioni Floreali in Sicilia', *L'Italia Agricola*, 103 no 5 (1966), 471–87

BIBLIOGRAPHY

GIARIZZO, A. 'Brevi Cenni sulla Cotonicoltura in Sicilia', *Bollettino della Società Geografica Italiana*, 95 no 6–8 (1958), 387–92

GUILOTTI, G. *Agrumicoltura Siciliana: Realtà e Prospettive* (Palermo, 1966)

MONASTRA, F. 'Produzione e Commercio Agrumario nella Regione Siciliana: Attualità e Prospettive', *Annali della Facoltà di Economia e Commercio dell'Università di Palermo*, 13 no 1 (1959), 127–72

PAGANO, L. A. 'Coltura della Vite e Produzione Vinicola in Sicilia prima del 1860', *Annali della Facoltà di Economia e Commercio dell'Università di Bari*, 5 (1951), 177–96

ROSSI, A. *La Viticoltura in Sicilia* (Palermo, 1955)

SPINA, P. 'Le Olive da Tavola in Sicilia', *L'Italia Agricola*, 103 no 10 (1966), 863–89

TAVOLARO, A. *Aspetti di Agrumicoltura Siciliana* (Catania, 1963)

TORTELLI, N. 'Foraggere e Bestiame in Sicilia', *Convegno Tecnico-Economico dell'Agricoltura Siciliana* (Palermo, 1960), 99–117

ZITO, F. 'La Frutticoltura Siciliana', *Convegno Tecnico-Economico dell'Agricoltura Siciliana* (Palermo, 1960), 88–98

In the journal *Monti e Boschi*, 14 no 11–12 (1963), 488–574 there is a collection of articles on Sicilian forests.

On fishing see the series of articles on Sicilian fishing ports in *Bollettino di Pesca, Piscicoltura e Idrobiologia*, 7–12 (1931–6); the articles on various aspects of the island's fishing economy in *Atti del 16° Congresso Geografico Italiano* (Padova–Venezia, 1954); also the following:

DELLA VALLE, C. 'Aspetti Geografico-Economici della Pesca in Sicilia', *Bollettino della Società Geografica Italiana*, 95 no 6–8 (1958), 399–406

STEIN, N. 'Die Fischereiwirtschaft Westsiziliens und ihre Auswirkungen auf die Siedlungs- und Bevolkerungsstruktur', *Frieburger Geographische Heft*, 8 (1970), 1–140

ZAHL, P. A. 'Fishing in the Whirlpool of Charybdis', *National Geographic Magazine*, 104 no 4 (1953), 579–613

References relating to agrarian unrest are:

BLOK, A. 'Land Reform in a West Sicilian Latifondo Village', *Anthropological Quarterly*, 39 no 1 (1966), 1–16

BOISSEVAIN, J. 'Poverty and Politics in a Sicilian Agrotown', *International Archives of Ethnography*, 56 (1966), 198–236

BIBLIOGRAPHY

BONFADINI, R. *Relazione della Giunta per l'Inchiesta sulle Condizioni della Sicilia* (Rome, 1876)

DIEM, A. 'An Evaluation of Land Reform and Land Reclamation in Sicily', *Canadian Geographer*, 7 no 4 (1963), 182–91

DI PAOLA, D. 'Assegnatari della Riforma a San Giuseppe Iato', *Quaderni di Sociologia Rurale*, 2 no 3 (1962), 48–52

DOLCI, D. 'The Chances of Full Employment Considered in Ten Sicilian Villages', *Community Development*, 2 (1958), 7–18

FAINA, E. ed. *Inchiesta Parliamentare sulle Condizioni dei Contadini nelle Provincie Meridionali e nella Sicilia* (Rome, 1907–11, 8 vols, especially vol 6 by Lorenzoni, G.)

FRANCHETTI, L. & SONNINO, S. *La Sicilia nel 1876* (Florence, 1925, 2 vols)

HAMMER, M. *Probleme der sizilienischen Agrarstruktur* (Basle, 1965)

JACINI, S. ed. *Inchiesta Agraria* (Rome, 1867–84, 15 vols)

LA BIANCA, U. 'Dall' ERAS all 'Ente di Sviluppo Agricolo' nella Regione Siciliana', *Collaborazione Mediterranea*, 11 no 1 (1966), 37–50

LA LOGGIA, E. *La Cooperazione in Sicilia* (Rome, 1951)

LONCAO, E. *Considerazioni sulla Genesi della Borghesia in Sicilia* (Palermo, 1899)

LORENZONI, G. *Trasformazione e Colonizzazione del Latifondo Siciliano* (Florence, 1940)

MEDICI, G. *La Distribuzione della Proprietà Fondiaria in Italia: Sicilia* (Rome, 1947)

MOLÈ, G. *Studio-Inchiesta sui Latifondi Siciliani* (Rome, 1929)

PONTIERI, E. *Il Tramonto del Baronaggio Siciliano* (Florence, 1943)

ROCHEFORT, R. 'Un Pays du Latifondo Sicilien: Corleone', *Annales Economies Sociétés Civilisations*, 14 no 3 (1959), 441–60

RUINI, C. *Le Vicende del Latifondo Siciliano* (Florence, 1946)

TARROW, S. G. *Peasant Communism in Southern Italy* (New Haven, 1967)

There is a wide and interesting literature on the Mafia, banditry and the *fasci*:

ALBINI, J. L. *The American Mafia* (New York, 1971)

ALONGI, G. *La Maffia* (Turin, 1877)

BOISSEVAIN, J. 'Patronage in Sicily', *Man*, 1 no 1 (1966), 18–33

BLOK, A. 'Mafia and Peasant Rebellion as Contrasting Factors in Sicilian Latifundism', *Archives Européennes de Sociologie*, 10 no 1 (1969), 95–116

BIBLIOGRAPHY

CANDIDA, R. *Questa Mafia* (Caltanissetta, 1956)
CHILANTI, F. & FARINELLA, M. *Rapporto sulla Mafia* (Palermo, 1964)
COLAJANNI, N. *La Delinquenza in Sicilia e le sue Cause* (Palermo, 1885)
————. *Nel Regno della Mafia* (Palermo, 1900)
CUTRERA, A. *La Mafia e i Mafiosi* (Palermo, 1900)
D'ALESSANDRO, E. *Brigantaggio e Mafia in Sicilia* (Messina, 1959)
DE LUCA, F. *I Fasci e la Questione Siciliana* (Milan, 1895)
FROSINI, V. 'Mitologia e Sociologia della Mafia', *Annali del Mezzogiorno*, 9 (1969), 367–83
GUARINO, G. 'Dai Mafiosi ai Camorristi', *Nord e Sud*, 13 (1955), 76–107
HOBSBAWM, E. J. *Primitive Rebels* (Manchester, 1959)
————. *Bandits* (1969)
KEFAUVER, E. *Crime in America* (New York, 1952)
LEWIS, N. *The Honoured Society* (1964)
MACK SMITH, D. 'The Peasants' Revolt of Sicily in 1860', *Studi in Onore di Gino Luzatto*, vol 3, 201–4 (Milan, 1950)
MAXWELL, G. *God Protect Me from My Friends* (1956)
MERCADENTE-CARRARA, T. *La Delinquenza in Sicilia* (Palermo, 1911)
MOLFESE, F. *Storia del Brigantaggio dopo l'Unità* (Milan, 1964)
MONTALBANO, G. 'La Mafia', *Nuovi Argomenti*, 5 no 6 (1953), 165–204
MORI, C. *Con la Mafia ai Ferri Corti* (Verona, 1932)
MÜHLMANN, W. E. & LLAYORA, R. J. 'Klientelschaft, Klientel und Klientelsystem in einer sizilienischen Agro-Stadt', *Heidelberger Sociologica*, 6 (1968), 1–52
NOVACCO, D. *Inchiesta sulla Mafia* (Milan, 1963)
————. 'Bibliografia della Mafia', *Nuovi Quaderni del Meridione*, 2 no 5 (1964), 188–239
PANTALEONE, M. *The Mafia and Politics* (1966)
————. *Antimafia: Occasione Mancata* (Turin, 1969)
REID, E. *Mafia* (New York, 1952)
RENDA, F. *Il Movimento Contadino nella Società Siciliana* (Palermo, 1956)
ROMANO, S. F. *Storia dei Fasci Siciliani* (Bari, 1959)
————. *Storia della Mafia* (Milan, 1963)
SANSONE, V. & INGRASCI, G. *Sei Anni di Banditismo in Sicilia* (Milan, 1951)
STERN, M. *No Innocence Abroad* (New York, 1953)

Two background works on vulcanism in Sicily are:

IMBÒ, G. *Italy* (*Catalogue of the Active Volcanoes of the World, Vol 18*) (Rome, 1965), 26–72

JOHNSTON-LAVIS, H. J. *Bibliography of the Geology and Eruptive Phenomena of the More Important Volcanoes of Southern Italy* (1918), 277–371

There are a number of thorough studies on Sicilian earthquakes:

ANDREWS, A. *Earthquake* (1963), 149–66

BARATTA, M. *La Catastrofe Sismica Calabro-Messinese* (Rome, 1910)

——. 'I Terremoti in Sicilia', *Reale Accademia dei Lincei Pubblicazioni della Commissione Italiana per lo Studio delle Grandi Calamità*, 6 (1936), 1–117

CARRÈRE, J. *La Terre Tremblante: Calabre et Messine 1907–8–9* (Paris, 1909)

HAAS, J. E. & AYRE, R. S. *The Western Sicily Earthquake of 1968* (Washington, 1969)

PLATANIA, G. *Il Maremoto dello Stretto di Messina del 28 Dicembre 1908* (Modena, 1909)

RICCÒ, A. 'Relazione Sismologica sul Terremoto del 16 Novembre 1894 in Calabria e in Sicilia', *Annali dell'Ufficio Meteorologico Italiano*, 19 (1897), 3–260

WRIGHT, C. M. 'The World's Most Cruel Earthquake', *National Geographic Magazine*, 20 no 4 (1909), 373–96

On other earthquakes and eruptions, see the volumes of *Bollettino della Società Sismologica, Bollettino dell'Accademia Gioenia, Zeitschrift für Vulkanologie*, and *Stromboli*.

Mount Etna is undoubtedly the most intensively studied feature in Sicily; Di Maggio, 43–54 and 259–65 has about 200 references on it. The main works of substance on the mountain are the following:

BORZÌ, G. *L'Etna nella sua Topografia, Mitologia, Vulcanologia* (Catania, 1904)

BUSCALIONI, L. 'L'Etna e la sua Vegetazione con Particolare Riguardo alla Genesi della Valle del Bove', *Bollettino della Società Geografica Italiana*, 46 (1909), 221–50, 369–400

CRINÒ, S. 'Bibliografia Storico-Scientifica della Regione Etnea', *Atti dell'Accademia Gioenia*, 4th Series, 20 (1907), 1–69

DE LORENZO, G. *L'Etna* (Bergamo, 1928)

HYDE, W. W. 'The Volcanic History of Etna', *Geographical Review*, 1 no 6 (1916), 401–18

BIBLIOGRAPHY

Imbò, G. 'I Terremoti Etnei', *Reale Accademia dei Lincei Pubblicazioni della Commissione Italiana per lo Studio delle Grandi Calamità,* 5 no 1 (1935), 1–94

Ponte, G. 'Riassunto delle Principali Osservazioni e Ricerche Fatte sull'Etna', *Bulletin Volcanologique,* 2nd Series, 9 (1949), 65–80

Rodwell, G. F. *Etna: A History of the Mountain and of its Eruptions* (1878)

Von Lasaulx, A. & Sartorius von Waltershausen, W. *Der Aetna* (Leipzig, 1880, 2 vols)

Finally, studies of individual periods of eruptive activity can be found in the following journals:

Annali dell'Osservatorio Vesuviano, 4 no 1 (1927–8), 293–384; *Atti Accademia Gioenia,* 5th Series, 4 (1911), whole volume; 6th Series, 11 (1956), 29–96; *Bollettino della Società Geografica Italiana,* 80 no 1–2 (1943), 20–9; 87 no 6 (1950), 323–34; *Bollettino della Società Sismologica,* 14 no 4–5 (1910), 141–205; *Bulletin Volcanologique,* 2nd Series, 9 (1949), 81–111; 2nd Series, 15 (1954), 3–70; *Geographical Magazine,* 44 no 7 (1972), 472–80; *L'Universo,* 27 no 5 (1947), 657–68; 40 no 5 (1960), 957–64; 46 no 4 (1966), 619–32; *Rivista Geografica Italiana,* 17 no 8 (1910), 393–403

Literature on Sicily's secondary islands is quite extensive and out of all proportion to the small areas and populations involved. A useful general survey is:

Mikus, W. 'Aspetti e Problemi della Geografia della Popolazione nelle Isole Minore d'Italia Meridionale', *Rivista Geografica Italiana,* 76 no 1 (1969), 15–52

On the Eolian Islands the most important works are:

Baldanza, B. *Guide for the Excursion to Vulcano* (Catania, 1961)

Bergeat, A. *Die Äolischen Inseln* (Munich, 1899)

Bernabò Brea, L. & Cavalier, M. 'Civiltà Preistoriche delle Isole Eolie', *Bollettino di Paletnologia Italiana,* 65 (1956), 7–99

——. 'Stazioni Preistoriche delle Isole Eolie', *Bollettino di Paletnologia Italiana,* 66 (1957), 97–151

——. *Il Castello di Lipari e il Museo di Archaeologia Eoliano* (Palermo, 1958)

——. 'Ricerche Paletnologiche nell'Isola di Filicudi', *Bollettino di Paletnologia Italiana,* 75 (1966), 143–73

Cavallaro, C. 'Filicudi', *L'Universo,* 47 no 6 (1967), 1015–56

BIBLIOGRAPHY

CICALA, A. 'Stromboli', *L'Universo*, 47 no 4 (1967), 601–26

CORTESE, E. & SABATINI, V. *Descrizione Geologico-Pedografica delle Isole Eolie* (Rome, 1892)

DE FIORE, O. 'Le Eruzioni Storiche di Lipari', *Zeitschrift für Vulkanologie*, 6 (1922), 114–55; 7 (1923), 1–54

——. *Vulcano* (Naples, 1923)

——. 'Bibliografia delle Isole Eolie', *Bulletin Vulcanologique*, 2 (1925), 113–61

DI RE, M. *Guide for the Excursion to Stromboli* (Catania, 1961)

GAMBI, L. ed. *Note ad Illustrazione delle Escursione Geografica Interuniversitaria nelle Isole Eolie* (Messina, 1955)

MARCUZZI, G. 'Aspetti Naturalistici delle Isole Eolie', *L'Universo*, 50 no 4 (1970), 915–36

MERCALLI, G., SILVESTRI, O., GRABLOVITZ, G. & PONTE, S. 'Le Eruzioni dell'Isola di Vulcano Incominciate il 3 Agosto 1888 e Terminate il 22 Marzo 1890: Relazione Scientifica della Commissione Incaricata degli Studi del Reale Governo', *Annali dell'Ufficio Meteorologico Italiano*, 10 (1888), 71–280; 11 (1889), 309–31

MIKUS, W. 'Vulkanische Inseln im Luftbild: Wirtschaftsgeographische Ubersicht über die Äolischen Inseln mit Hilfe von Luftaufnahmen', *Die Erde*, 100 no 2–4 (1969), 71–92

PERINI, G. 'Recenti Modificazioni Antropogeografiche nelle Isole Eolie', *Rivista Geografica Italiana*, 77 no 4 (1970), 393–430

PERRET, F. *Report of the Recent Great Eruption of Stromboli* (Washington, 1913)

SALVATOR, L. *Die Liparischen Inseln* (Prague, 1893–6, 8 vols)

SICARDI, L. 'Il Recente Ciclo dell'Attività Fumaricola dell'Isola di Vulcano', *Bulletin Vulcanologique*, 2nd Series, 7 (1940), 85–139

SPERANZA, F. *L'Isola di Salina: Studio Geografico-Economico* (Catania, 1953)

STURIALE, C. *Guide for the Excursion to Lipari* (Catania, 1961)

ZAGAMI, L. *Le Isole Eolie nella Storia e nella Leggenda* (Messina, 1939)

——. *Lipari e i suoi Cinque Millenni di Storia* (Messina, 1960)

On Ustica there are:

BONASERA, F. 'L'Isola di Ustica', *Annali della Facoltà di Economia e Commercio dell'Università di Palermo*, 17 no 2 (1963), 1–42

SALVATOR, L. *Ustica* (Prague, 1898)

TRASELLI, C. *Il Popolamento dell'Isola di Ustica nel Secolo XVIII* (Caltanissetta, 1966)

BIBLIOGRAPHY

On the Egadi Islands *see*:

DE MAURO, M. 'Solitudine di Marettimo', *Vie d'Italia*, 73 no 11 (1967), 1308–20

FRANCINI, E. & MESSERI, A. 'L'Isola di Marettimo nell'Archipelago delle Egadi e la sua Vegetazione', *Webbia*, 11 (1956), 607–846

GRAZIOSI, P. 'Le Pitture e Graffiti Preistorici dell'Isola di Levanzo nell'Archipelago delle Egadi (Sicilia)', *Rivista di Scienze Preistoriche*, 5 (1950), 1–43

SALERNO, F. P. 'Le Isole Egadi', *L'Universo*, 39 (1959), 159–72, 739–52

Three recent studies of Pantellaria are:

BONASERA, F. *L'Isola di Pantellaria* (Bologna, 1965)

GIRONE, E. *L'Isola Disperata: Pantellaria* (Milan, 1946)

TOMASINI, G. 'Pantellaria', *L'Universo*, 45 no 4 (1965), 551–62

INDEX

INDEX

INDEX

206

INDEX

Page numbers in italic refer to illustrations